WEALTHY SEEDS

A Guide to Wealth, Health, and Knowledge of Self

Terrance "Sun God" Wells Jr

Foreword by Graytz "Self Power" Morrison

ISBN: 978-1-09836-152-5 Print
ISBN: 978-1-09836-153-2 eBook

CONTENTS

Dedication 1

Acknowledgements 3

Preface 5

Foreword by Graytz "Self Power" Morrison 9

Introduction 19

Part One: Student Enrollment (1-10) 21

Part Two: Lost Found Keys to Success (1-14) 29

Part Three: Nourishment for Thought (1-36) 39

Part Four: Knowledge Your Culture Cipher (1-40) 45

Part Five: Actual Facts (1-20) 87

Glossary 111

Appendix: Notes 117

About the Author 125

DEDICATION

To my mother, you are my strength.

ACKNOWLEDGEMENTS

I humbly express my gratitude to everyone's input, insight, and/or inspirations that helped me complete this literature. A special appreciation for those who dealt with my difficultness upon giving me feedback for this project. Sometimes a person knows enough to think that he is right but not enough to know that he is wrong. There are a lot of people who supported this project but I am only going to name the ones who were critical to its completion: Matthew "Knowledge Born Allah" Thompkins (my enlightener), Graytz "Self-Power Allah" Morrison, Raoul "Great" McFall, Ronnell "Ron Du Allah", Blaine "JuJu" Gamble, Logical Thought Allah, Tyshawn "Nino" Jones, Bro. Matata Askari, Summel "URO" Sutton, Eric "E" Erskine, Gale "Big guy" Green, Sean "Pretty Tone" Lambert, Nasim "True King" Burton, The Nation of Islam and The Nation of Gods and Earths. Also, The Mississippi Library Commission staff: thank you for all the information. Peace

Cover Design by Amy T. Ziegler
Cover Illustration by Kyam Natural Bakari

PREFACE

At the time of this writing, I do not have any physical seeds (Children) and I am not wealthy (in a financial sense). However, I am wealthy in intellectual and social currency. I possess supreme knowledge that allows me to think in abstract patterns and mathematical sequences, which gives birth to mental conceptions that I can monetize by fortifying my universe with the right friendships. My failures have enabled me to succeed more than anything else. The brightest moments in my life manifested out of the darkest times.

When I see the condition of my people it causes severe pain to my soul. The 155 years that we have been free in this country, individually we have made profound accomplishments and contributions, however the totality of the black nation here in the wilderness of North America has made little progress since the civil war. A harsh but true reality. A small percent of us have prospered in this nation but the majority are suffering. We lack the power to overcome the affliction because we are not precise in the study of self.

Our culture has been taken from us and was replaced with a way of life that is not parallel with our nature. We have been living in this un-natural state for so long that we believe that its normal.

A wise person believes until they take their beliefs through mathematics. If their beliefs measure up to math, then they no longer believe they know. Most of my people believe in a culture and system that is not in harmony with mathematics. Belief without traveling the course to know is the root of our powerless condition.

I have composed 120 questions and answers of wealth health and knowledge of self. This is a guide to building wealth mentally as well as physically. Using math, science, and real-life success stories. I have constructed a merit base formula to cultivating mental gold that enables you to manifest supreme intelligence into something tangible of greater value.

My writings only contain 120 degrees. Mathematics teaches you that you need 360 degrees to be complete (circle). So, this information alone is just foundational knowledge to get you to look, listen, and observe things for what they are and not what they seem to be. Some of this info you might view differently and that is ok. I encourage you to take the best and leave the rest. Utilize what you understand by planting wealthy seeds in the fertile- soil of the mind. It is up to you to water the useful land to manifest the other 240 degrees.

Black people are the original people of the planet earth. original means (origin in all). Your ancestry can be traced back to energy, matter and thought. We are the fathers and mothers of civilization.

The short period of time that we have been mentally and physically poor is minuscule compared to the thousands of years that we were the wealthiest people on the planet. Society will tell you otherwise, they must, it is how they keep us powerless. People will tell you that these lessons are false and to disregard them. Will you take what they say on face value? Or will you study and research to know truth?

I am part of a culture that teaches me to study the science of everything in life. Through my intense studying I have developed the ability to understand things clearly with my mind which is my third eye. As I continue to study, my understanding evolves. I have a duty to teach to the degree of my knowledge. Once I enlighten you with the precious jewels of life, my obligation is fulfilled, it is up to you to take the jewels and make jewelry.

I am asking you to take this information and study it, measure it and add on. Make it applicable to your circumstances and CHANGE YOUR CONDITION. Then teach the people around you. **SUNGOD AMENTI**

FOREWORD

by Graytz "Self Power" Morrison

In this present date of our existence, we do not have to live in the past to understand our great history and apply lessons from it. We know that we must add some things and subtract some things, this is simple math. Mathematics is not a belief or theory; it is a compilation of facts through repeated observations using trial and error but what we do not know and should know is that we as human beings are the highest form of mathematics and must learn how to separate factual information from subjective content. We must thoroughly observe the facts in order to become more in tune with absolute reality.

In early stages of development when our children' minds are most impressionable there should be heavy emphasis placed on them learning the value of themselves and the value of the earth. They also need to learn how and why the black legacy has been trampled upon and regarded as primitive heathenism, thus non-contributory to world civilization.

The unified black family should not only know about the great accomplishments of America and Europe. They should know about the great accomplishments made by the people of African/Alkebulan decent and their impact on world civilization through the original migration periods. We should also teach ourselves and our children etymology and basic understanding of the original languages like Medu Netcher, the language of ancient Kemet (Egypt) which translates to words of the divine, and some derivatives of the originals like Arabic, Greek, and Hebrew. So now we can place proper perspective on what we read by identifying pseudoscience, misnomers, interpretations and/or outright plagiarism. Then we can begin to figure out why the mother land home of the original man and woman came to develop over 2000 different languages and dialects and why there is so much war, hatred, and slavery in and against predominately black societies. If we plant the proper seeds (wealthy seeds) into the mentally fertile minds of our children beginning at kindergarten ages, they will then grow and develop within the facts of black contribution. We can better equip them with the ability to see importance within themselves; thus, allowing them to strive to find answers to modern black and human problems through studies like migrations in and out of Africa. A perfect place to start with these studies would be the human genome project which was done by national geographic. This project gives us many links to the first migration periods. These same ideals were expressed by The Legendary Rapper – Nas, in his song 'Africa must wake up'…"We cannot be afraid of who we are today, we are the morning after the makeshift, youth the slave ship captured our Diaspora in the final chapter, ancestral linage-built pyramids, Americas first immigrants, the Kings sons and daughters from the Nile waters, the first architects, the philosophers, astronomers, the first prophets and doctors was us"…

Because of rape and pillage through Asian, Arab, and then European conquest and the continued disunification amongst blacks all over the planet, contributions made by blacks on world civilization have evaporated into a fine mist that the naked eye can hardly detect. Moreover, with most blacks disoriented of time, space, and geography and hoping for social equity; we have been easily misdirected and manipulated into disrupting black progress to this very day. When one thinks through a clear and free perspective, he/she should no longer operate through orthodox nor speculative views, as they understand that history as told by its conquerors has not been good natured nor truthful when it comes to black people. When I speak of black, I speak of it synonymous with people who contain significant amounts of melanin. It is my hopes that readers do not misconstrue my thought process and know that I understand that growth order and development of all children is important regardless of color and/or geographic origin. But we all know that the black child is the most neglected. should we not note that the black child sees their self as inferior to other races and ethnicities. It should not be forgotten that Black America is a subculture or by product of European conquest.

"A whole generation does not respect themselves which makes it easier for them to shoot each other. This is a generation of kids who do not have father figures. They are looking for their manhood and they got a gun" (john singleton movie producer 1968-2019) (1)

Thus, some of these reasons are why black children should be taught about their true origins. The scientific properties of melanin are why their hair is so curly and the differences scientifically about straight and curly hair. They also should be taught about what defines race, nationality, and ethnicity. Also, when, and why these concepts came about. Why do we vehemently neglect the study of ourselves? The study of self gives parents clear lenses and a real foundation to build off. The study of self enables us to teach our children in a manner that empowers and inspires one to add on positively to the world, thus destroying the negative aspect. Sometimes, both Black and White parents allow their children to be blind followers of history instead of researching the people themselves. The naivete of the parents has a harmful effect on the minds of the children because they grow up viewing themselves and their history through the eyes of men in the likes of philanthropist Charles Loring Brace, Professor Samuel G. Mortan, scientist Francis Galton, and imperialist Cecil Rhodes. Whose school we are so eager to send our children to in order to receive a Rhodes scholarship. Although, not negating that these colleges offer great benefits if one is looking to make advancement in his/her field of studies. However, we must not abandon critical thought on the complexity of the ideology of Europe and America consolidated into textbooks and accepted by most of the world. Google these men so that you can better understand how the black inferiority complex continues to perpetuate itself 155 years after slavery and why these late historians defiled our blackness.

"The 4th of July- memorable in the history of our nation as the great day of independence to its country man had no claim on our sympathies." "They made a flag and threw it to the heavens and bid it float forever; but every star in it was against us". Henry McNeal Turner Bishop, Civil Rights Activist. (2)

It can be debated, I believe, but modern scholars state that Black America has always been a nation within a nation, and they say we that identify with black have yet to realize this reality. With the passing of the 13th amendment in 1865 blacks were freed from physical slavery and the U.S. Constitution. In 1868 blacks were re-introduced back into the Constitution under the equal protection clause of the 14th amendment as citizens of the united states. This turned out to be another slap in the face because with the passing of the 14th amendment came the Ku Klux Klan (KKK), white unions, black codes, poll taxes, and Jim Crow, which morphed into heavy investments into the building of prisons and a war summoned against blacks. Moreover, the 13th Amendment did not completely end slavery, it made slavery exception for those convicted of a crime. Consequently, we have been identified as felons/criminals and deemed 2nd class citizens. They switched the language. Instead of calling you a slave they call you a felon or criminal. Blacks have been disproportionately targeted by laws that brand them felons. Though Black people are no longer legally hung from trees; we are now lynched in state and federal court rooms through unfair legal litigation. Thus, the historical energy towards blacks being less than human is rendered cyclical because we know that energy did not die, it just changed forms.

"Black people know what white people mean when they say law and order"(Fannie Lou Hammer; Civil Rights Activist 1917-1977). (3)

Great books to read dealing with these unjust laws that have plagued us are: The New Jim Crow by Michelle Alexander and Dr. Claud Andersons, Black/Labor White/Wealth. These books show and prove why we still deal with injustices and why they lay out strategies on how to identify inherent unjust policies, while giving reference to solutions that can possibly free us from the tyrannical practices of the dominant society that has refused to be held accountable for tactics that have kept Black people at the lowest rung of the socioeconomical ladder.

"No one has ever heard the Jews publicly chat a slogan of Jewish power, but they have power." "Through group identity, determination, and creative endeavor they have gained it…" "This is exactly what we must do" Martin Luther King Jr 1929-1968) (4)

Since our forced introduction into this land, we have been socially abused to the point of being numb to the abuse and as a result many of us have come to accept the inferior mentality that the slave master forced on to us. With this reality, it seems impossible to rise above our social and economic ills. There will always be sprinkles of black success.

They are the ones who were strong enough to survive the life taking wrath of America and still be ambitious enough to make it through that narrow window of opportunity. The rest of us fell victim to the barriers of this civilization. The sad but true fact that even blacks who sincerely fight for the best interest of the United States get discriminated against and willfully excluded as unimportant. For example, former President Franklin D. Roosevelt's highly regarded New Deal policies, which encompassed many government funded wealth building programs including the G.I. Bill which passed legislation in the 1930s intended for war veterans, gave veterans access to mortgages with no down payments and helped catapult millions of working-class veterans into college and new homes. Thus, creating the so called "middle class". This was not very much so for black people. Blacks were actively excluded from the above benefits because of the discriminatory application of the G.I. Bill although the G.I. Bill did not explicitly exclude black war veterans, racial discriminatory tactics endured in the form of the veteran administration that embraced the same racially restrictive policies as the federal housing administration, which guaranteed bank loans only to developers who would not sell to Blacks. The new deal along with the G.I. Bill helped save the housing market but actively excluded Black neighborhoods from government insured loans…

"Gentrify your own hood before these people do it, claim eminent domain and have your people move in" Jay-Z (5)

Webster dictionary defines black as wicked, evil; of or relating to African American people or the culture. It cannot be said enough that we, Black people, were shaped by the actions of dominate society and did not name ourselves negro, ni***r, colored nor black as these labels were applied to us by the dominate society and under U.S. Constitutional law, black people were once considered a dead people.

"I am societies child, this is how they made me, and now I'm saying what's on my mind and they don't want that." "This is what you made me America" Tupac Shakur (6)

When put into proper context black is known to be the direct descendants of creation original man and woman made manifest in the physical form thus the fathers and mothers of civilization. We have walked the earth through every phase of human evolution, therefore; with this understanding, the negative connotations associated with blacks are dealt a severe blow when viewed through unaltered scientific lenses. Black people have shown and proved their natural magnetic attractiveness in a plethora of ways omnipresent in every culture whether good or bad.

Through my intense study of history, my thoughts magnetically attract to the minds of leaders like Booker T Washington, Marcus Garvey, Kwame Nkrumah (understudy of the late Patrice Kumumba), Elijah Muhammad and Dr. Claud Anderson because history which bears witness to many great lessons shows and proves that the greatest opportunities that blacks had were the ones, they have created for themselves. Accordingly, these men have created opportunities, blueprints and/or strategies for black progress and generational wealth. However, it is up to us to come together and make these plans work.

We need collective works and a lot less ego. We need to form a mindset that benefits the whole of our neighborhoods, thus, recreating community sense. Group economics must be established. We must create a system where we control production of goods and services all the way to the distribution. We must set pride to the side and work through our differences. The rich, the poor and the so-called middle class must work and struggle as one to liberate the whole. We must establish links locally and nationally through black industries in urban areas. A great place to start this process would be through social media. Black people as individuals, their churches and other community-based organizations must move to a #usnowornever movement.

Everything in America is for sale and everyone is racing to buy and fix up deteriorated neighborhoods except for Black people. We must have the same control on the collective level that we strive for on the individual level. I is self and self is the consciousness of one's own being, so I is especially important, but we are also a piece of the whole. Happiness will only come from what we produce from the sum of the whole.

"The thing to do is to get organized; keep separated and you will be exploited, you will be robbed, you will be killed." "Get organized and you will compel the world to respect you" (Marcus Garvey 1886-1940) (7)

Our history expands the entire 196,940,000 square miles of this planet. We are the cause and effect of everything in existence. History flows in a cyclical motion like a clock. So, the studied must learn and teach others how to master the clock... Not only are we the inventors of the clock but we ourselves are the measure of its' time. All great leaders who established movements or causes that moved humanity forward knew their history. They studied the history and related it to modern times. They measured present day circumstances against historical events of the past which developed a foresight that enabled them to dictate the future. No mystery involved just an active mind on history and the time.

"History is a clock that people use to tell the culture and political time of the day." "It is also a compass that people use to find themselves on the map of human geography." (John Henrik Clarke, Historian 1915-1998) (8)

When we as fathers and mothers fail to review, study, and renew our history; we create a miscarriage of justice for our children. If we continue to allow schools to teach our children their history, it will only lead them to see themselves no further than the slave ship. Their subconscious views of who they are will be distorted. We must study our history and apply what applies to free ourselves and our families from our mental state of unawareness. In conclusion, it is in my hopes that you enjoy this read, as it is intended to enlighten, uplift, and compel our people toward the unlimited possibilities of mental and physical wealth.

I love you and always remember that positive education always corrects errors.

Graytz "Self Power" Morrison

"Change will not come if we wait for some other person or some other time." "We are the ones we've been waiting for." "We are the change that we speak." Barack Obama (First African American President 2009 – 2017) (9)

INTRODUCTION

*When I say " What's the Science " it is a way of asking—did you know this? And I will show and prove my methods of how to do something or give factual basis surrounding a subject while breaking it down to a science.

Thoroughly study my thesis and disregard anything not compatible with math.

Disclaimer: This is not a new interpretation of the 120 lessons utilized by the Nation of Islam and the Nation of Gods and Earths. The structure and life giving teachings of the lessons were an inspiration and a road map for me to bring you this material.

PART ONE:

Student Enrollment (1-10)

Student Enrollment

1. Who is the Poor Person?

The Poor Person is one who desires to be fed with what falls from the rich persons' table. A person who lacks knowledge, wisdom, and understanding and has no concept of fasting, budgeting, nor planning.

2. Who is the Rich Person?

The Rich Person is one who works to acquire large sums of money but is not mentally equipped to make large sums of money work for them.

3. Who is the Wealthy Person?

The Wealthy Person is one who views the world from a mathematical perspective and understands the science of economics. The Wealthy Person obtains capital, assets, and resources that are used to cultivate an economical base for the survival and prosperity of all human families on the planet earth.

4. What is the median net worth of all white families in North America?

$171,000. A large percent of their wealth is inherited. (1)

5. What is the median net worth of all Black families in North America?

$16,600. 3/4 of the wealth is held in the family car, meaning the Black family is really worth around $4,000. Nineteen percent (19%) of Black families have zero or negative net worth. (2)

** *What's the Science* **

A 2016 report by the Institute for Policy Studies found that if the average Black family's wealth grows at the same pace as it has over the past

3 decades, it would take 228 years to amass the same amount of wealth that white families have today. Today's median wealth of white households is nearly 10 times higher than Black households and 8 times higher than Hispanic Households. (3)

Financial wealth does not happen by accident or overnight. It takes planning, commitment, and discipline. The wealthy see money as employees who work 24/7 without breaks or vacations. The un-wealthy see money as friends who provide temporary gratification.

6. How do we close the gap between Black and White family's wealth?

By making education our first investment. We must teach our children knowledge of self. We must teach them the science of training for success in the battles of life. We must teach the mathematics to wealth-building to our children and pass down our culture so they respect and understand where they come from, so they can lead us to where we need to go.

7. Why do so many Black kids drop out of school?

Because the curriculum that is being taught to Black children is a paradigm that advocates the concept that the Black child is inferior to the white race. Therefore, they cannot see themselves in the teachings except as slaves to mental death and power...

The parents are the first teachers of the child. Other than preschool, a child's first exposure to education outside of the home is kindergarten. Kindergarten is a German word. The etymology of the word is kinder=child, garten=garden (4). So, kindergarten means (child garden). America knows that a child's mind is (kind of like a garden) so they use the school system as one of their many tools to plant seeds in the useful land of the child's mind. However, no matter how fertile the soil, you can never grow the tree of life from a pumpkin seed.

These early years of school are the most sensitive. The images impressed on the mind of the child will design and control the consciousness of one's own being. Therefore, when white children learn about the Great men who founded America or Great minds such as Einstein or Thomas Edison, they can see themselves in the teachings. So, they grow up with feelings of superiority that give them confidence and self-pride that enables them to prosper because all their life they have been taught that they are the cream of society.

The schools teach the Black children about these same great men of America, but it has an adverse effect. The teachings only show Black people as inferior, so the child develops an inferiority complex which usually causes them to lose interest and drop out or they continue to travel through the educational system that's more about the system than education with a weak mind state that accepts the illusion that Black people are inferior. If the Black children learned about how they are descendants of the original people of the planet earth and that their ancestors invented music, sports, hunting, spoken language, writing, math, science, and countless other things…

They will develop a self-pride that will enable them to succeed in life because they will know their potential is limitless.

** *What's the Science* **

The miseducation the Black child receives at schools, most of which are named after the slave master and with teacher who share the slave master's views, play a key role in the child's inferior mentality.

"The potter is responsible for the shape of the clay, so be careful who you let mold the mind of your babies."

8. What is cooperative economics?
The science that deals with the production, distribution, and consumption of wealth by the pulling of resources for the collective advancement of a community:

E - Educating
C - Communities
O - On
N - Networking
O - Our
M - Money
I - Intelligently
C - Cooperatively
S - Successfully

9. Why is the Blackman incarcerated 6x more than the White man? (5)
Due to the lack of growth, order, and direction, the Blackman becomes a product of his environment instead of making his environment a product of him. He has been subjected to a powerless reality that created an illusion that the only upliftment from his condition is to commit violations that go against his nature and the laws of society...

The Blackman is incarcerated at a higher rate because he begins life from a disadvantage. If we look to the recession of 2008 as a recent example of how certain demographics bounce back from economic hardship, the picture becomes clearer...

** *What's the Science* **

Did you know that in 2017 white home ownership rate reached 72.9% up from 72.2% the year earlier? Black home ownership fell to 43%, the lowest rate since the Fair Housing Act in 1968. (6)

Home ownership is one of the fundamental pillars of building wealth. The financial crisis of 2008 initiated an enormous destruction of wealth for Black people because they were hit disproportionately hard by the housing collapse and unable to rebound like other demographics (despite a strengthening economy, including record low unemployment and higher wages for Black workers). This is a direct effect from discrimination in real estate, biased policies, and lack of financial knowledge.

** *What's the Science* **

The McKinsey Global Institute (MGI) did a research report on America's racial wealth gap. It found that Black families are underserved and over-charged by institutions that can provide the best channels for saving. For instance, banks in predominately Black neighborhoods require higher minimum balances ($871) than banks in white neighborhoods do ($626). Unsurprisingly, 30 percent of Black families are underserved by their banks, and 17% are completely disconnected from the mainstream banking system because of a lack of assets and a lack of trust in financial institutions.) (7)

Sometimes people make bad decisions, not necessarily because they're a bad person, but more likely because they have been put in a bad situation for generations. (The Blackman's fear of staying in poverty forever is far greater than his fear of incarceration, so the opportunity to obtain fools' gold will make risk factors obsolete.)

10. What is the Greatest obstacle that a person must overcome to succeed?

Oneself...

YOU are the obstacle that stagnates your progress and growth...

Despite the harsh realities and barriers that society imposes to create and continue to expand the racial wealth gap. You still have the power to control your outcome. Inequities, turmoil, and pain are a part of life, but it doesn't have to define you. One must search within instead of without because the power comes from within. Examine self and take ownership and responsibility for your decisions. Identify your weaknesses and improve them. One must have a vigorous desire to change one's condition which develops ambition.

(He is a great man who conquers self than he who kills a thousand men in war - Buddha)

PART TWO:

Lost Found Keys to Success (1-14)

Lost Found Keys to Success

1. How you react to failure:

"Your life will be defined by how you react to failure."

In the pursuit of success, failures and setbacks will occur. You must make failures matter by learning from your mistakes and approach obstacles with boldness, self-assurance, and mental fortitude. That will enable you to succeed or fall and get back up and try again with confidence.

"If there's no struggle, there's no progress." - Frederick Douglass

2. Circumstances x Reality = Destiny:

Circumstance - a fact or event, one accompanying another or conditions affecting a person, esp. financial condition. (1)

As a child you're not able to control the circumstances that you are born into. As a parent you have the POWER to dictate the circumstances, conditions, and environment by which your child is surrounded. Parents must maximize the opportunity to shape their children's' future by building wealth and passing it down. When children are born into a functional family where their foundation is (Health, Wealth, and Knowledge of Self) it bolsters their chances to attain their dreams and aspirations. (This is the first step to building generational wealth).

Reality - is something that really exists. Fact of being. (2)

Fact: The racial wealth gap continues to increase due to socioeconomic inequities.

Black Americans' 'racialized disadvantage' which was created by historical tactics to keep Blacks on one side of economics (consumers) which denies Blacks the opportunity to build a nation of producers. Also, poor, and disadvantaged peoples' lack of exposure to investing, saving, and overall financial knowledge plays a key role in the wealth gap.

The absence of equality in the economic system of this nation is advocated with full awareness of its stagnating effect on Black people on this poor part of the planet Earth.

Destiny - State or end that seemingly has been decided beforehand. (3)

When you're thrust into this world into the hands of a dysfunctional family and environment, your CIRCUMSTANCES begin to cripple you. Multiply that by a society that has an economical structure that was designed to oppress, enslave, and keep people poverty-stricken.

When this is your REALITY, it creates a fear of poverty that becomes so great that it will force you to go against your nature to survive. Even if it means destroying your own people and yourself. Therefore, your DESTINY becomes incarceration, addiction, or death!

3. Keep Your I's over your E's!
(I = Intelligence, E = Emotions)

One thing most successful people have in common is that their reasoning remains stronger than their emotions.

Set your emotions aside when navigating through the hills and valleys of life. Make decisions on what's best for the people/community, rather than for personal gains.

Keep your I's over your E's when doing business unless your Emotional Investment is bigger than the business. "Keep Ya I's over Ya E's God" Self-Power Allah

Before you speak: listen, before you consume: invest,

Before you spend: save, before you quit: TRY HARDER!

4. Change your thinking, change your condition.
Always think positive!
"Everything you thought about you didn't do, but everything you did, you thought about."

Everything begins with a thought. What are you thinking?

Watch your thoughts: they become language; watch your language: it becomes actions.

watch your actions: they become habits; watch your habits: they become culture,

watch your culture: it becomes your destiny.

5. Do for self:
We are divided by race, culture and religion, but we are one people…"I want for my people what I want for myself. So, if I do for my people, I do for myself."

Madam C.J. Walker was one of America's earliest Black female entrepreneurs. She was the pioneer of the hair care and cosmetics industry for Black women. She is famously known for saying, "I got my start by giving myself a start." (4)

She credits her success to diligence and hard work. Also, she said, "I am not merely satisfied in making money for myself, for I am endeavoring to provide employment for hundreds of women of my race." (5) She wanted for her people what she wanted for herself. She understood that economics and education are key elements in the upliftment of her people.

6. Know that it is you who will get you where you want to go:
Good things come to those who wait. Great things come to those who make Great efforts to make Great things happen!

"Don't let anybody tell you that the sky is the limit when you're the creator of the universe."

7. Leadership and Innovation:
Leaders show and prove with their ways and actions. Leaders provide empowerment, moral courage, and vision.

Leaders practice "we not me" by surrounding their selves with capable people, steering them in the right direction and creating a free-thinking culture, which enables them to achieve optimum results...Great leaders are innovators. They introduce new ideas, methods, and disrupt industries.

Jordan Peele disrupted Hollywood with his debut film "Get Out," which he earned an Oscar for Screenwriting and a nomination for Best Director. On just $4.5 million budget, the film grossed a quarter billion dollars worldwide. (6) It exceeded all expectations. The movie industry has an aristocratic origin that still exists today with its lack of diversity on every level. Peele challenged this state of normality, by showing and proving to the world that a movie written by, about, and starring Black people can be a major success.

8. Embrace the GRIND!
"A soldier without a foe never knows his strength." - Moorish Holy Koran (Circle 7) Proverb

As you navigate through life you encounter hurdles and hardships. As you overcome these obstacles you will develop an ability to recover from or adjust easily to misfortune or change. This is an essential skill needed for one to succeed. A person who does not come face to face with adversities early on in life, in not mentally equipped to sustain existence.

Billionaire Robert F. Smith, most recently known for paying off graduates' debts at Morehouse College in Atlanta was resilient on his path to success. During his speech at Morehouse, he stressed the point that throughout his years of being a chemical engineer, he spent almost every waking hour in windowless labs doing the work that helped him become an expert in his field. He said, "only after I put in the time to develop this expertise and the discipline of the scientific process that I was able to apply my knowledge beyond the lab." Also, he said, "Greatness is born out of the grind. Embrace the grind." (7)

As of 5-20-19, Forbes put R.F. Smith's net worth at $5 billion. He is the richest Blackman in America. He achieved this status because of his resilience and profound drive.

9. Tomorrow belongs to the hustler who prepared for it today:
Never put off for tomorrow what you can do today. Without determination, fortitude, and a profound drive you won't make it.

Most people put things off until the last minute. What they do not realize is that this is becoming a habit. When you wait until the last minute to do small things like work around the house, the affect is minimal. However, this character trait is exhibited in everything you do, so when you have a deadline at your job, you will probably wait until the last minute to do it because you have created a bad habit. This affect might not be minimal, it could result in you getting fired.

10. Social currency:

Wise is the person who fortifies his life with the right friendships.

In Silicon Valley former employees of prominent start-ups like Air BnB, lift, and Uber are creating tech mafias (8) (networks of alumnae from the companies) who support, hire, or invest in their peers' new businesses. Silicon Valley has a perception that it's a meritocratic society, (but in reality), it's a small close-knit club where success usually depends on who you know rather than what you know...

90% of cofounders of Fortune 500 Companies had at least a few years working together or knew each other from college. Think about the college scam that numerous celebrities were caught up in. (9) Already successful and wealthy people paying large sums of money to inflate their children's SAT scores to get them admitted into prestigious schools because they understand that some of the people who are shaping the world went to these schools and the chances to make connections can be just as priceless as the education they provide.

11. Your WORD must be bond:

A person's word must be impeccable. There are very few things on this earth worse than a liar.

12. Cultivate your mind:

cultivate - Growth and development. Refinement of your true culture.

Mind - The seat of consciousness. The root of civilization where undeveloped thoughts need proper cultivation to reach a Supreme state.

"More gold has been mined from the thoughts of men than has ever been taken from the earth." Napoleon Hill

Cultivate your mind with a life-giving education that allows you to reach your full potential. not only just a college education but study yourself. If you don't know who and what you are, you'll never know when you have reached your apex.

"Education is the gateway to freedom from mental and physical poverty."

The correlation between education and wages shows that the higher educational level a person attains the higher the wages.

A person who has a bachelor's degree will earn 40% more every week on average than someone who has a high school diploma.

Part of cultivating your mind is being conscious of the fact that just by being Black there's social and economic inequities that stand in the way of prosperity. Add 'under educated' to the equation and your chances of making it out of poverty are small.

13. Know what you want to accomplish:
Set specific and realistic goals, then take the proper steps necessary to achieve them.

Set simple short-term goals to create a habit of accomplishing your goals, so when you set complex goals, you'll be comfortable and confident in accomplishing them.

The key to succeeding is your goal being realistic. You can't set a goal to make a billion dollars in one year. 99.9% of the time you're going to fail. (Patience is a virtue): very few people have microwave success. It's an unrealistic approach.

Also, align yourself with productive and capable people who see your vision that will help you achieve your goals.

14. A seed goes down first, before it goes up!

Struggle + Patience = Power

struggle - to make great efforts; strive; labor. (11)

Patience - Enduring pain, trouble without complaining; calmly tolerating delay, confusion, diligent; persevering. (12)

Power - Truth and energy living according to the truth. (Vigor; force; strength)

The most effective self-transformation comes from experiencing pain from mistakes and using the pain as motivation to succeed.

There's a very thin line between letting the pain shatter your ambition and using it as motivation to continue the course of action despite difficulties.

One must keep their composure and have a willingness to endure the struggle to develop a state or quality of being strong. Never wanting to feel the pain again fuels the motivation to succeed.

"POWER IS TRUTH"

The strength converts to power when you struggle and learn the truth about yourself and your goals. Only then will you possess the power to take on every force in the universe (including oneself) that stands in the way of financial freedom.

Look, listen, and observe things for what they are instead of what they seem to be, because the struggle allows you to learn and grow.

People who avoid struggle also avoid success.

PART THREE:
Nourishment for Thought (1-36)

Nourishment for Thought

1. My name is SUNGOD AMENTI and I fast and eat to live.

2. What is fasting?

3. Fasting is the voluntary abstinence from all food and drink except water, for an extended period.

4. How could I go days without eating? Is that safe?

5. Your body by nature is designed to fast.

6. What are the benefits of fasting?

7. Fasting is the universal healer of all ills both mentally and physically. Fasting extends your life.

8. How does fasting extend my life?

9. The bad foods we consume both mentally and physically are the root of all illnesses. Fasting is one of the most effective and safest ways to strengthen your mind and immune system, which extends life.

10. But what about the people who don't fast or eat to live, that live longer than average?

11. The leading causes of death in this country such as heart disease and cancer are direct results of unhealthy diets.
Most people of color in America have or are at high risk of chronic diseases. This is due to our unhealthy dietary habits. The few people who eat unhealthily and live longer than expected are miniscule compared to the millions of people who die young from unhealthy eating.

12. What is the safest and most effective way to fast?

13. I recommend a water only fast for at least 24 hours once per week. Then extend how you see fit.

14. How do you eat to live?

15. By eating less. The human body is not equipped to handle the American diet of high protein animal foods and processed products 3 times a day. I recommend a plant-based diet.

16. What is a plant-based diet?

17. A diet high in whole grains, fruits, and vegetables (no animal flesh). Also, for ideal nutrition, I recommend low fat, low protein, and low sodium.

18. Did I hear you say no meat?

19. Yes, most of our population has been nutritionally miseducated. Animal based diets are linked to chronic diseases and overall bad health.

20. But what about protein?

21. The human body is not designed to function on a high protein diet.

22. Is protein harmful?

23. Protein from animal products have a negative effect on your health. Consume low amounts of protein from non-flesh products, ex. beans or oatmeal.

24. How does plant-based diets effect your health?

25. Plant based diets and fasting have a positive effect on your health. They have been proven to increase longevity, also a successful approach to treating and recovering from diseases and injuries.

26. So the saying, "you are what you eat" is true?

27. Yes, when you consume food (mentally and physically) that gives and sustains life, you live long. Consumption of the wrong foods shortens your life.

28. What is your method of fasting?

29. Water only, for 48 hrs. straight every week. And every 13 weeks I extend the fast to 72 hours.

30. How long have you been doing that

31. For the last 2 years and I plan to do it for the rest of my life.

32. What are the exact days and hours that you fast per year?

33. 108 days and 2,592 hours per year. At this rate, in 20 years I will have fasted a little over 5 years and 10 months.

34. What other benefits do you receive from fasting?

35. Mental fortitude and clearer thinking; also, I feel light.

36. Food is one of the pleasures of life. Food is also one of the hardest things to turn down. When you can go without food for extended periods or change your diet to mostly consist of healthy foods, you create a discipline that's priceless. Mental fortitude allows you to channel this discipline to every facet of your life.

To build wealth these same qualities are necessary. So, when it comes time to decide of whether to save or spend; invest or buy something you want; sacrificing will come easy because fasting and healthy eating has conditioned your mind to choose needs over wants.

*** Peace ***

PART FOUR:

Knowledge Your Culture Cipher (1-40)

Knowledge Your Culture Cipher

1. Tell us why planning and budgeting is essential to wealth accumulation?

Planning and budgeting are allocating your funds effectively to maximize your future financial growth. Wealth planning and budgeting are the financial building blocks to cement your future. They are essential to acquiring wealth because a wealth plan lets you see the bigger picture, a budget helps you keep your eyes on the prize.

Employ the 3-bucket system: now, soon, later

NOW: Covers living expenses and emergencies that arise.

SOON: Investments

LATER: Retirement

2. Why is saving so important?

Strong savings and modest living pave the way to financial freedom.

Working couples should sacrifice and live modestly off one income and save and invest the other income. Eating at home more often and taking less vacations are sacrifices that make living off one income more sustainable. Saved money can be used to pay debts down such as school loans or mortgages. Real estate and Exchange Traded Funds are good low risk investments.

** *What's the Science* **

While the top 10% of families by income saw average savings rate increases for the past 3 decades, the bottom 90% of families by income saw negative savings rates, contributing to higher debt levels (1)

3. Why must people in poverty learn the value of credit and financing?

"Because the knowledge of credit and financing are the vehicles to economic empowerment."

Credit is everything. Not using it properly will keep you in debt and debt is the mother of poverty. Bad credit makes it hard to get loans for housing, investments, or vehicles. If you do get a loan the interest rates will be extremely high which will push you further into debt. Credit is measured by FICO scores. FICO scores range from (300-850). Having a credit score of 680 and above allows you to qualify for lower interest rates on loans. When your credits are good, you're able to get financing for investments, which is what you use to control an asset using a small down payment. Benefits of financing are the ability to invest in multiple properties, magnify returns, and become wealthy much faster.

When you credit is optimal, banks will 80% finance you, which means if you want a $100,000 loan you only need to put down $20,000 (20%) and they will loan you $80,000 (80%).

4. Tell us why wasting dollars don't make cents?

"The loss of a dollar is more than a dollar loss, it's the loss of the potential that dollar could have made."

When you ask people why they don't save more or put the max amount in their 401(k) plans the most common answer is "I don't make enough," but they waste money daily on small dollar purchases like coffee, bottle water, and snacks…

If you don't spend $3.50 on coffee, $1.50 on bottle water, and $2.00 on snacks per day you'd save $2,555 a year. If you invested that money over

30 years, you'd have over $200,000 (with a 6% annual interest rate of return).

** *What's the Science* **

Did you know that large cap stocks (companies with 5 billion or more in market value such as apple, amazon, and Walmart) average an annual gain of 10.14% from 1926 through June 30, 2019? (2)

5. Tell us why money is a great servant but a wicked master?
Money is a servant who recruits other servants (more money) to collectively work together to generate more money when invested proficiently.

When money is your master, you're being ruled by something outside of yourself which forces you to go disaccording to your nature and moral principles. This usually leads to a state of imperfection instead of a state of happiness.

6. What Is Compound Interest?
Compound interest is earned interest reinvested. Ex. If $100 is deposited into a bank account with 10% annual interest, the depositor will have $110 at the end of the first year and $121 at the end of the second year. (3)

7. How Much Money Is Sufficient for Retirement?
Estimate how much money you spend annually and times that by 35.

** *What's the Science* **

Did you know that if a person invests $500 a month with an average annual return of 8% in 35 years, they'll have $1.1 million

Depending on your lifestyle, this may or may not be enough for retirement. People who procrastinate with saving and investing while they're young will jeopardize the financial security of their retirement.

A good retirement plan is especially important. You must think for the future of your family and yourself. You can still enjoy life on a lesser budget. Take advantage of the gig-economy. Cut down living expenses, and be willing to work 2 jobs, so you can max out your 401(k) and Roth IRA. The goal is to build up a large enough nest egg that you can withdraw 4% per year in retirement without touching the principal.

8. What Is the Said Prescribed Laws of Investing?
Allocating assets among stocks, bonds, and real estate.

An investor should compose a strategy based on their perspective of interest rates, inflation, and economic growth. Also consider the investor's age, tolerance for risk, and amount of capital available to invest.

Investing in index funds such as exchange traded funds (ETF) and mutual funds are effective ways to maximize gains and minimize risk.

** *What's the Science* **

Apps that make it easier to save or invest:

ACORNS: A micro-investing app that rounds up debit and credit card purchase to the dollar, directing extra pennies into diversified portfolios of (ETF's).

CHIME: Mobile-first bank offers checking accounts, debit cards, and services that rounds up purchases, depositing extra pennies in savings. Members can tap into direct deposit pay two days early with no fee.

ROBINHOOD: Offers commission-free trading of stocks, ETF's, options, and crypto currencies through a mobile app and online.

STASH: A mobile app that offers commission-free and fractional purchases of stocks and ETF's themed investment portfolios and IRA's. Users with less than $5000 pay $1 a month, others pay 0.25% of asset a year.

9. Will You Please Define Debt and Show Us the Proper Way to Use It?

Yes, debt is money, goods, or services that one party is obligated to pay another in accordance with an expressed or implied agreement.

There are 2 types of debt:

GOOD DEBT: Borrowed money invested into income producing assets that enable one to pay back loans and still profit. Ex.: Real estate, businesses, or merchandise.

BAD DEBT: Borrowed money incurred to purchase things that depreciate or hold little value. Ex. cars and clothes.

"ONE WHO IS BOUND BY DEBT IS BOUND TO FAIL"

Debt is the enemy of success. For it becomes your master because it possesses the power to stagnate one's financial growth for generations.

When you have debts i.e. (student loans, mortgages, or credit card bills) financial institutions rarely give you loans because they feel that you're over leveraged. If they do, it will be at a high interest rate which will cost you thousands of dollars over time.

THE CHART BELOW COMPARES THE CORRELATION BETWEEN FICO SCORES AND INTEREST RATES: LOAN AMOUNT $500,000. TIME 30 YEAR MORTGAGE.

FICO	APR	MONTHLY PAYMENT	INTEREST
720-850	5.3%	$2752.73	$494,549
700-719	5.9%	$2965.68	$567,647
680-699	6.5%	$3160.34	$637,722
620-679	7.6%	$3530.37	$770,937
560-619	8.4%	$3809.19	$871,305
500-559	9.9%	$4350.95	$1,660,352

The chart clearly shows how low FICO scores can keep a person in debt. By getting a 30-year mortgage on a $500,000 property you would pay 3 times as what the property is worth, with a (500-559) FICO score. A million dollars more than a person with a (720-850) FICO score.

Eliminating debt helps increase your credit score, which allows you to get the best interest rates, deals, and sometimes not required a down payment or collateral when applying for loans. One must learn the science of budgeting. It's the key to establishing economic empowerment. Most people's expenses exceed their income. You must learn to live within your means. Decide what your essentials are such as food, clothing, and shelter. Then make them priority and remove the things that are unnecessary.

Apps that help you budget:

EVEN: A budgeting and savings mobile app that links to users' bank account, asks about upcoming bills and estimates how much they have left to spend. Employees can pay $8 a month to get access to money they've already earned ahead of pay day.

10. What Is the Danger of Living Paycheck to Paycheck?
Many Americans are living paycheck to paycheck and are not financially secure to face an unexpected crisis, such as job loss or death in the family.

In 2019 the economy was booming. The stock market hit record highs and unemployment was at a record low. However, many Americans are living on the fringes of poverty because they were excluded from the boom due to their lack of stock and home ownership. With rising expenses for education, healthcare, and housing, it's difficult to save or invest when you live paycheck to paycheck. Emergencies happen unexpected. Put yourself in a position to be prepared for setbacks.

** *What's the Science* **

65% of self-made millionaires have 3 streams of income, 45% have 4, and 29% have 5 or more. Having multiple streams of income are essential to wealth building. We live in a society where the cost of living out paces most 9 to 5 wages, so to counter inflation one must have a full-time job, a side hustle, and a part-time job. (4)

11. Why Must Your Weapon of Choice Be Financial Knowledge in the Economical War Being Waged Against the Middle and Lower Classes?

"Because financial literacy is the common component in all who holds wealth"

The rich are the controlling class of the wealth. The U.S. economic growth has slowed as inequality has increased. Of the world's major developed economies, the U.S. is among the most unbalanced. There is a massive disparity in wealth and the gap is getting wider. Wealthy people spend a smaller portion of their income on goods and services than middle- and lower-class people. They're more likely to invest or save their money. The richest 1% of Americans own about half the stock market.

The middle and lower classes lack of investing and saving is a large part of the disparity in wealth. Also, the lack of education and skills to get the high paying jobs of the future.

** *What's the Science* **

Did you know that the fastest growing 6-figure job in America is an application developer? The median salary is $101,790 a year. Even more mind-blowing is that it's degree optional. App developers who build and update computer and mobile apps can major in computer science at any 2- or 4-year program, but most go to coding boot camps. Boot camps are vocational schools devoted to creating software developers. They're unconcerned with SAT scores, diplomas, or background in computers. Students need only 2 things: a grasp of logic and driving ambition. Most have venture capital backing and accept a share of the graduate's first year earnings or a finder's fee from employers as payments.

Recommended boot camp: (Tech Elevator)

Tech Elevator is a 14-week coding boot camp and career prep program, teaching people with a variety of backgrounds to become software developers and land fulfilling careers in tech.

Program combines expert instructors with passionate career coaches and helps you connect to who you are, and where you want to take your career in tech.

14-week program, full time, Mon-Fri, 9a-4:30p

Financing available

on-site employer matchmaking

Program site: Cincinnati, Cleveland, Columbus, Detroit, Pittsburgh, Philadelphia (5)

Knowledge is the key to freedom from debt and poverty, regardless of your color or class.

An economical system of knowledge will enable you to hurdle over roadblocks.

12. Create your own L.U.C.K (laboring under correct knowledge) Bro Nuri Mohammad (6)

Tristan Walker of Walker & Co. brands created his own L.U.C.K.

Walker grew up in a single parent home in the housing projects in Queens, N.Y. Statistics say that he had a better chance of going to prison than getting an Associate's degree. However, despite the odds he surpassed all expectations. His mother who understood the correlation between education and wealth instilled in him a passionate commitment to learn. Also, she worked 3 jobs to set him up for success. He went on to attend Stony Brook University and graduate school of business at Stanford. He excelled in school because he was resilient in his pursuit of knowledge, but most importantly he learned how to apply the knowledge that he obtained into making himself an entrepreneur instead of an employee. After graduating he went back home to work on Wall Street and soon realized that he hated it. "I felt that the world was bigger and that there were other things that needed solving" (7) Walker said in an interview with the New York Times. He was all wise and mature which gave him the ability to reject good alternatives to pursue more vital aspirations. He quit Wall Street and started a consumer goods company. One of the problems he wanted to solve was the lack of adequate beauty products for people of color. Shaving was always a problem because the products irritated his skin. He realized that most people with curly hair had the same issues. Being that people of color will be the majority by 2040 and they spend more money on these products than anybody, he felt that the demographic was being neglected. So, he founded Walker & Co., a maker of health and beauty products for people of color. Products that cater to their needs and celebrate their culture. After successfully running the company for 5 years, it was acquired by Procter & Gamble, the maker of Gillette.

He came up with a unique and valuable vision and built it into a beautiful company. However, becoming a successful entrepreneur was just part of his plan. He went on to cofound Code 240, a nonprofit that nurtures black and Latino tech talent. He understands that it's a drastic demographic shift happening in America. In 20 years, people of color will be the majority. While at college in Silicon Valley he saw a lack of diversity in the tech world. It was a close-knit society that people of color were excluded from. He saw young people making millions of dollars and changing the world. He wanted this opportunity for his people. So, he Labored Under the Correct Knowledge (L.U.C.K) by walking away from Wall Street to pursue more meaningful endeavors with the purpose of providing efficient products that respect the culture and community of people of color. Also, by succeeding and coming back to open doors for his people to succeed.

13. Have you heard that learning to do without when in need, creates a discipline that is essential to wealth building?

Nobody wants to be cheap. There's nothing wrong with buying nice things in moderation when you can afford it. Some people are fascinated with name brand objects. These things bring temporary status and pleasure. What people are oblivious to is the harmful long-term effect of spending recklessly. Some people have thousands of dollars' worth of shoes and clothes but have (zero) dollars in their bank account.

You always hear about how some of the wealthiest people live the most modest. They don't drive extremely expensive cars or wear excessive jewelry. They dress casually. Their clothes are that of a person who works in a warehouse but (in reality) they are the CEO of a Fortune 500 company. This is because they understand the value of money. Along their pursuit to wealth, they developed a habit of making good decisions with money and once they obtained wealth, they didn't abandon their principles. Making good decisions with money is the core element in obtaining and sustaining wealth.

14. What are the said laws of attraction?

You will attract to you people who are like-minded and harmonize with your philosophy of life whether you wish it or not. So, use this law to attract people to you who will help you achieve your goals...

A fact of life is that you become like those with whom you strongly associate with. The laws of nature also exhibit this same principle: (women who live in close proximity and are constantly around each other will find that their menstrual cycles begin to synchronize) (8). When you are striving for success like-minded people will recognize this and gravitate toward you.

Great relationships are a major part of reaching success, because when you surround yourself with prosperous and accomplished people, you are able to utilize these relationships to achieve your goals. Also, by fortifying your life with successful people you will learn and absorb qualities and characteristics of what it takes to be successful.

15. Is hard work the only component one needs to achieve financial success?
Emphatically no. Hard work alone is not sufficient to carry a person through to financial success. Financial success is the result of discipline, fortitude, and entrepreneurship. "Success brings wealth and in order to become wealthy in America as a minority you must equip yourself with many weapons" Knowledge Born Allah

As a minority you need to be disciplined to sustain the valleys and peaks of life while keeping your financial goal a priority. You need fortitude to display the mental toughness it takes to make hard decisions. (Working a job can prepare you for the battle but entrepreneurship wins the war). As a minority in America, you have a lot of uphill obstacles to overcome to attain wealth. Entrepreneurship is the tool for which you use to maneuver through the obstacle course.

Discipline x fortitude = sacrifice

Sacrifice means to forfeit one thing for another thing thought to be of greater value. Nothing in life holds more value than life itself. So, you must sacrifice temporary desires in the present to preserve life for the future. Preserving life for the future means saving, budgeting, and long-term planning. These things enable you to build wealth and pass it down to future generations. It's hard for someone in their twenties to see 20 years down the road, but this type of vision is quintessential to success. One must have patience and be willing to make sacrifices that are conducive to a financially secure future.

16. When is it too late for you to change your life?
Never! Every successful person failed, but every person who failed didn't succeed!

"You don't drown by falling in water, you drown by staying there."

A decision made in 20 seconds could cost you 20 years of your life. That shows you the power of your decisions. When this is fully understood, you'll know that it's never too late to change because when you (change your thinking you change your condition.)

Maurice Smith spent (27) years in prison. He made some bad decisions early on in life, but he didn't let those decisions define his future. In 1992, Smith was sentenced to life with the possibility of parole for murder. At the young age of 19 he was thrust into a hostile prison environment which usually swallows up young men. Instead of giving up on life, he enrolled in college courses and made the dean's list.

In 1994 President Clinton signed a crime bill that took away Pell Grants for prisoners. So, Smith, frustrated that he could no longer take college courses became angry and bored and began to get in trouble. He spent years in and out of solitary confinement.

In 2012, the Goucher Prison Education Partnership began operating with private donations. In 2013, after serving over 20 years Smith realized that he would be getting released soon so he started to pursue a degree at Goucher. All he did was sleep, study, and work in the kitchen. His profound drive and intellect enabled him to graduate with a 3.79 (GPA). After being released in 2019, Smith was able to attend the graduation ceremony. His classmates who were more than 20 years younger than him embraced him with great respect.

Smith currently works at a warehouse. When asked about his job he said, "My education could never be accurately valued by the pay I receive at my job." There is infinitely more value in the way in which I now view the world. (9) Smith made mistakes early on in life but never gave up. His story is an inspiration for people who think it's an age limit on success.

17. What is the said duty of a wealthy person?
The said duty of a wealthy person is to teach the financially illiterate the science of economics, investing and philanthropy otherwise known as love, peace, and happiness.

(Eddie Brown the founder of Brown Capital said in an interview "it's incumbent upon those of us who are of color in the investing field to do everything we can to spread the word that this is an area of tremendous opportunity to create wealth," "also it's not just about wealth but to be in a position to then do something good for others.") (10)

Brown was born in Apopka, Florida in 1940. He grew up in the Jim Crow south in a town without paved roads, indoor plumbing, or electricity. Despite the oppression and the obstacles that society placed in front of him, he still succeeded beyond racial parameters.

At age 43 he started Brown Capital an investment firm that currently holds over $12 billion in assets. He credits his success to his family for teaching him entrepreneurship. His uncle taught him how to drive at the age of 6, so he could help drive the truck while his grandfather worked in the fields. His grandmother preached education and the teachers at his segregated school instilled in him that as being black in America you're going to have to be twice as good to make it.

Brown's actions showed that he fully understood this because he did excellent in high school and applied to Howard University and was accepted. An anonymous woman paid for his tuition, room, board, and books. After graduating from college, he held a couple jobs and then decided to go to business school.

In 1973 the president of T. Rowe offered him a position at the prestigious firm. He accepted and became the first Black portfolio manager in Baltimore. In 1979 he began appearing regularly on the iconic weekly PBS show: Wallstreet with Louis Rukeyser. The exposure from the show led him to start his own firm. In 1983 Brown Capital was founded. His first account ($200K) came to him via a letter sent to the show. It was President Johnson's former personal secretary Geraldine Whittington, the first African American to work in the White House in that role.

The firm hunted for unattractive but fast-growing companies. This counterintuitive approach made the firm an extremely successful stock picking operation. Brown's innovative thinking helped the firm exceed expectations. In 2016, Brown completed an employee stock ownership plan, meaning his 36 employees (70% of them minority) now own the Baltimore firm. This move was a result of him being bothered by the recent closures of African American owned firms.

Now a centimillionaire by Forbes estimate, Brown is giving away his money, inspired by his anonymous benefactor who paid his tuition. Over the past 25 years Brown and his wife distributed close to $40 million to dozens of educational, religious, and artistic endeavors...

When you understand economics, you know that Black people are the #1 consumers, and we spend 95% of our money outside of our communities. (11) Our buying power is $1.2 trillion, more than most countries GDP. (12) Therefore, we miss the benefit of group economics. Our ignorance of economics is the bridge for which other cultures cross to get to wealth. Love correlates directly with economics because when you love your people you build businesses in your community. Also, the people from the community spend their money with the local businesses because they put the money back into the community. This is the first step of economic development.

Investing is a vital part in building wealth. By investing $800 a month in an index fund that earns a 10% annual rate of interest, in 40 years you will have over $5 million. $800 a month is a lot especially when 20.8% of Black people live below the poverty line. (13) However, these same people spent $473 million on hair care products in 2017. (14). This clearly shows that Black people have the power to change their condition by simply making wise investments (education, stocks, real estate) instead of wasting money on things that hold no value. When this is grasped mentally you live in a state of tranquility and righteousness, which is peace.

Happiness is good health and prosperity. With this enrichment comes a great desire to help others. The wealthy person has a moral obligation to pass down knowledge and donations to the babies who are the future.

18. Why does America keep us apart from their economic equality?
Because they are afraid that when we learn the science of economics
we will produce and build for ourselves. Therefore, we will no longer
be dependent on them which is the key to them possessing 95% of the
wealth. (15)

The late Nipsey Hussle was far more than just a great rapper. He was
also the savior of his community. Nipsey learned the science of economics and used the knowledge to change the culture of his people.

He possessed the courage, vision, and ability to guide his people to economic freedom from poverty-stricken communities. He understood
that getting an education that teaches entrepreneurship was essential
to freeing his people from the chains of poverty. He started Vector 90
a large working space in the Crenshaw District of LA, that caters to
the economic development of the people in the community. Vector 90
is a program that helps its members build businesses from the ground
up. Also, it offers (S.T.E.M) classes for children. The demand for jobs
in the technology sector is higher than the supply. Our children need
to be equipped with these skills to obtain the high-paying jobs of
the future. In reference to the (S.T.E.M) classes, Nipsey said, "in our
culture, there's a narrative that says, 'follow the athletes, follow the
entertainers...'"

And that's cool but there should be something that says, "follow Elon
Musk, follow Mark Zuckerberg." (16)

Nipsey was a generational leader. What he did for his community will
change the trajectory of Black families forever and needs to be implemented in all Black communities on the planet Earth. Nipsey didn't live

to see the fruits of his labor but he planted seeds in the minds of the children who will grow into the trees of life.

R.I.P Neighborhood Nip

19. Will you tell us why it's important for the parent to be a living manifestation of what they teach to the children?
"The culture and character of the child is sown with the thread of the environment and the people who live within."

Tope Awotona is the founder of Calendly, an online scheduling company. (17) he encountered many stumbling blocks along his journey to success. Awotona credits his upbringing in Nigeria and his family for instilling in him a foundation of entrepreneurship, education, and resilience. His grandmother built a remarkably successful import-export textile business. She also owned many homes and sent all her children to college. His mother worked 2 jobs. When she wasn't working at the Central Bank of Nigeria, she was working at the pharmacy which she co-owned with his aunt. His father was a micro-biologist who quit his job to start his own business.

Awotona's family showed and proved with their ways and actions how to build wealth despite their circumstances. When Awotona was 12 years old he watched his father get murdered in a carjacking—tragic but common occurrence in Nigeria. He felt that his father died before completing his work, so part of his drive to succeed was to redeem him.

In 2013, he launched Calendly. Initially he (boot strapped) his business to get it off the ground but he soon ran out of money. He needed investors so he went to venture capitalist for funding but was unable to raise money. He encountered the common problem all Black founders face when seeking VC funding: rejection. He had a working product with customers and VC's still were unwilling to invest. Even more discouraging, he saw other people who fit a different "profile" get funding for inefficient ideas. Due to the hostile environment, he grew up in and the independent culture his family passed down; he was mentally equipped to manage this situation. Instead of giving up he embraced the grind and became more resourceful, strategic, and learned to use money more efficiently. His diligent effort resulted in him being the majority owner of a business that's approaching 30 million in recurring revenues.

20. How much does our planet weight?

The Black woman is symbolic to the Earth because she is the Mother of all human life. The Earth weights 6 sextillion tons. The weight of

the earth correlates with the load, burden, and responsibility that the Black woman has to carry. The Black woman faces the greatest obstacles throughout life, but her DNA is built to survive and overcome anything the universe throws her way.

All women encounter great obstacles on their pursuit of wealth in this male-dominated society. However, we must deal with the fact that the load on Black women is much heavier than any other women.

The Black woman faces a dual repression. Not only does she experience racism, but she faces sexism in a white male dominated world.

The chart below shows the weekly wages by education for Black men, Black women, all men, all women. It clearly shows a racial and gender disadvantage for Black women.

Black Weekly Wages by Education

2018 Median earnings per week *(employed full time)*

	Black	all USA
ALL EDUCATION LEVELS (25yrs & up)	$715	$909
Less than a High School diploma	$483	$515
High School graduates, no college	$599	$718
Some college, no degree	$661	$774
Associate degree	$707	$836
Bachelor's degree only	$933	$1,189
Advanced degree	$1,188	$1,451

	Black Men	all men
ALL EDUCATION LEVELS (25yrs & up)	$727	$995
Less than a High School diploma	$504	$583
High School graduates, no college	$653	$797
Some college, no degree	$711	$886
Associate degree	$790	$978
Bachelor's degree only	$998	$1,375
Advanced degree	$1,295	$1,732

	Black Women	all women
ALL EDUCATION LEVELS (25yrs & up)	$707	$824
Less than a High School diploma	$450	$444
High School graduates, no college	$539	$620
Some college, no degree	$624	$680
Associate degree	$649	$727
Bachelor's degree only	$897	$1,030
Advanced degree	$1,133	$1,270

SOURCES:
U.S. Bureau of Labor Statistics
U.S. Census Bureau
2018 Current Population Survey

BLACK
DEMOGRAPHICS
BlackDemographics.com

After a quick look at the chart, you'll notice that Black women with associate degrees only earn $66 more per week than all men without a high school diploma. This racial and gender disadvantage shows that it's still a serious problem within the economic structure of this country. Education correlates with higher wages but not always equal wages.

** *What's the Science* **

When it comes to women owned businesses, Black women face a heavily unbalanced economic playing field. (A 2018 American Express report for women-owned businesses showed that the average revenue for businesses owned by Black women in 2007 was $84,100; by 2018 it had dropped to $66,400. Businesses owned by White women in 2007, the average revenue was $181,000; by 2018 it had jumped to $212,300.

This disparity is mostly because of systemic racism and sexism when it comes to getting funding or loans. Therefore, it's vital for successful Black entrepreneurs to create funds and invest in the most precious natural resources on this earth (The Black Women). (19)

Richelieu Dennis entrepreneur and owner of Essence launched the New Voice Fund, a $100 million fund to invest in businesses owned by Black women. In an interview with Inc. magazine, he said "we're trying to solve a problem. And that problem is something like 7 cents of every dollar in this country goes to women of color businesses. With that disparity, our communities are never going to be self-sustaining." (20)

21. Tell us why ignorance is your worst enemy?
Ignorant: 1. without knowledge or education; 2. oblivious, unaware, unconscious; 3. not aware or informed. (21)

Illiterate: having little or no formal education. Ignorant of the fundamentals of a given art or branch of knowledge. (22)

Enemy: 1. one feeling or displaying hostility or malice toward another foe; 2. A hostile force or power; 3. something having destructive effects. (23)

The destructive effect that ignorance plays on our people is not only stagnating our growth and progress as a nation, but it's the foundation for which billion-dollar industries are built on. Many of which who advocate for laws or policies to exclude people of color from economics.

Stagnation is death. We are a mentally dead people. We must wake up and draw the power from within to change our condition.

The wealthy person reads more than one watches TV. The poor person watches TV more than one reads!

Benjamin Franklin once said, "An investment in knowledge pays the best interest."

This is true. One must make the investment in the knowledge of oneself but know that the path of knowledge is an infinite path. The reason for our condition is that we strayed?? away from that path and started taking what society said on face value. We're the architects of the universe. That's a fundamental principle of life, that has been exhibited throughout history and even today we are still shaping the world.

22. Why must Mother Earth guard the mind of the babies?
The mother must learn the science of how to activate the God potential within the DNA of the child. For the babies must be fed the proper nourishment one needs to sustain existence to manifest and evolve this supreme force. The mother must guard the mind of her babies by first being extremely cautious of what she allows to be ingested into her psyche. For her thoughts are the first writings on the babies' brain. The mind of the child is crystallized by the mental and physical foods of which she intakes.

The environment possesses the ability to mark and shape the baby because hostile conditions or surroundings place strenuous pressure on one's emotional, mental, and physical wellbeing. Therefore, tension grows within the womb. When a baby receives the proper nourishment, they learn and think at light speed. The adverse effect directly correlates with poverty because unhealthy eating, thinking, and living produces unhealthy babies who will more than likely have learning disabilities and psychological disorders. Even though many of us overcome these harsh circumstances, most of us are devoured by them.

Higher education associates with higher income and higher incomes are associated with greater life satisfaction. Lower education associates with lower income and lower income associates with poverty and crime.

** *What's the Science* **

- 18% of Black men 25 and up did not complete high school compared to 14% of all men. (24)

- About 6% of Black males age 18-64 are currently in a state or federal prison or in municipal jails 3x higher than (the 2%) of all men in the same age group. (25)

- Although incomes for African Americans have improved since the civil rights era, they are still lower than the national average. For ex., the median income for Black families ($49,549) is 20K less than the national median income ($73,891). (26)

- Black Americans can expect to earn up to 1 million less than White Americans in their lifetimes. (27)

23. How much are you willing to sacrifice to achieve success?
"To achieve success, I'm willing to sacrifice my rest, my personal down-time, and any other time outside of my woman and my babies. you must have balance. Your family, woman, and babies provide the stability needed to keep you grounded. Sacrifice is good only when it's done for the greater good of all involved." Knowledge Born Allah (28)

To achieve success, one must make a commitment to sacrifice but on your pursuit of financial freedom, never surrender the things that money can't buy. Wealth is the ability to fully experience the pleasures of life with the ones that you love. So, make the appropriate sacrifices in the present in which their long-term effect is for the greater good of your family and future generations.

24. Why does the habit of saving foster every virtue needed to build wealth?

Because it's not how much money you make it's how much money you keep. What keeps most middle-class families stagnated in the middle is that they lack the foresight to see the fruits for which grows from sacrificing now. This type of long-range thinking cultivates success in any endeavor.

Many millennials are becoming members of the growing (F.I.R.E) movement (Financial-Independence-Retire-Early). They're making six figures a year and are saving and investing 70% of the income. The key is to keep a tight budget on food, clothing, and entertainment. Also max out your IRA or 401K contributions every year. (29)

Investing and saving requires a rare discipline as society puts an enormous amount of pressure on a person to live a certain type of lifestyle. Being frugal with money is extremely hard, especially with social temptations with friends or co-workers. Passing up opportunities to go out for drinks or wearing out of style clothes is a humbling experience. Friends might call you cheap or stingy. The ability to reject good alternatives to pursue a greater purpose builds maturity and empowerment.

25. What is the said principle that successful entrepreneurs live by?

The Flair Principle: Fail, Learn, and Improve, Rapido.

The Flair principle is a systematic way to approach the path to becoming a successful entrepreneur.

Fail: fail-means to fall short, to be unsuccessful in something.

"The only person who has never failed is the person who has never tried."

That basically means that failure is inevitable, it's how you react to it that determines whether you become successful or not.

The first step in becoming a successful entrepreneur is having a great idea and knowing what you want to accomplish. Whether you're building a product or providing a service you must take the necessary steps to manifest your idea from a vision to reality.

This process involves putting your idea on paper and then translating it into a product or services. Once the translating is complete you test it to see how it works.

At this stage most people get discouraged and give up if things don't work exactly how they envisioned it.

Learn: learn means to gain knowledge or understanding of or skill in by study, instruction, or experience.

To learn from failure, you must first admit that you failed. Re-evaluate your methods and formulas to put you on a path with a greater probability of success.

When the experience of failure is thoroughly studied you gain a great understanding of why you failed which develops the ability to succeed. Learning from mistakes allows you to re-approach the situation with the benefit of hindsight. Thomas Edison once said, "I have not failed. I've just found 10,000 ways that won't work." This quote is an example of an extraordinarily successful person possessing the ability to walk from failure to failure without losing enthusiasm. This is an ability that's essential to success.

Improve: Improve-means to enhance in value or quality; make better, to advance or make progress. Improvement is the progress made by learning from failure after fully comprehending the circumstances of why you failed. Examine the test stage and study feedback. Listen to the market, they'll tell you why you failed. Often failure is the result of an inadequate team, lack of financing or ineffective leadership. These steps must be done "Rapido" (which means quickly in Spanish) to increase your chances of succeeding.

Fact: Black people receive the smallest percent of venture funding. So, financing will always be a roadblock. Black people must take advantage of the things they can control, like being an effective leader and building a team of capable people who believe in the vision and have a profound drive to accomplish it. Black people must be twice as good to receive the same opportunities offered to other people. And this is ok because success tastes sweeter when it's born out of the struggle.

** What's the Science **

Harlem Capital Partner (HCP) is a New York-based early-stage venture capital firm, that is on a mission to change the dynamics of the funding world. HCP has a groundbreaking goal: to invest in 1,000 diverse founders over the next 20 years.

The firm was launched by managing partners Henri Pierre-Jacques and Jerrid Tingle in 2015. "We fundamentally believe we are a venture fund with impact, not an impact fund." Pierre-Jacques told Tech Crunch. "The way we generate impact is to give women and minority entrepreneurs ownership." According to RateMyInvestor and Diversity VC report released early 2019, most VC dollars are invested in companies run by white men with a university degree. Other data indicates that the median amount of funding raised by black female founders, as of 2018, was $0! (30)

One of the main reasons this problem exists is because most VC funds only invest in people who look like them and have similar backgrounds. It's our responsibility to invest in our own people. Firms like HCP are quintessential to Black wealth.

26. Will you tell us why the culture of the teacher can make a significant difference in the academic achievement of our children?
Research shows that when black and Hispanic students have teachers who match their ethnicity, they have higher test scores, graduation rates, and college attendance. In my opinion this is partially because teachers of color provide a relatable experience to the student of color that transcends what they learn with pencil and paper. This relatable experience comes from the cultural understanding of the teacher which is often absent from public schools.

The culture of the teacher is not only significant from preschool through 12th grade, but it also matters at the college level. Consider Historically Black College Universities (HBCU).

HBCUs provide a unique opportunity for black children to be educated by teachers who look like them and understand where they come from. Black parents must understand how vital it is for the babies to be in comfortable environments, around people they can relate to for them to learn and grow at a proper pace. The lack of diversity at predominantly white colleges makes most black children feel out of place and uncomfortable. Therefore, black students' graduation rate is notably higher at HBCUs. Also, HBCUs produce 80% of black judges, 50% of black doctors, 40% of black engineers, 40% of black members of Congress, 13% of Black CEOS. (31) Therefore, they are responsible for nurturing the black middle class.

Graduates from HBCUs who go on to become successful must use their wealth and influence to uplift and empower black communities by supporting and advocating for children to attend HBCUs.

** What's the Science **

Did you know that nearly 280 hate crimes were reported in 2017 to the FBI by select campus police departments, up from 257 in 2016 and 194 in 2015? The FBI collects hate crime data from a much smaller sample of colleges than does the Education Department. The largest year to year increases in hate crimes reported to the FBI in terms of motivating bias, occurred in crimes against multiracial victims, African Americans, and Jews. (32).

The Anti-Defamation League's center on extremism found that incidents of white-supremacist propaganda had increased at America's colleges in the 2017-18 academic year by 77% from the year before. (33)

27. Why is it important for the seeds to be cultivated with an education that enables them to be self-sufficient?
Our children need a foundational education that places them on the highway to financial freedom. Most children go to college and get an education that they're not equipped to use to build wealth. After college, most graduates are now working in the fields of their major. If they are, their debt for the education is much greater than their income.

In 2017 at USC, students who earned a master's degree in Drama and Theater Arts owed $100,796 at graduation but earned just $30,800 in their first year. However, science and engineering majors show the exact opposite. At MIT, Math majors earned a median of $120,300 after graduation, while borrowing just $8,129. The lowest debt to income ratio for bachelor's degree. (34) An investment in S.T.E.M has the highest return.

What you go to school for plays a major role in your pursuit of wealth because student loans are stagnating people financially for generations.

28. Why is S.T.E.M education essential to life?
(Science - Tech - Engineer - Mathematics)
We must put our babies in position where they can get a proper education that gives them the tools to manifest their own opportunities throughout life. We must provide a field of study that produces the capabilities to provide for one's own needs. Most of our people have skills that are only applicable to jobs that will be obsolete in the future. Or jobs that have limited advancement. We must become independent. Build our own businesses and become employers instead of employees. S.T.E.M education provides this opportunity.

Hadi Partovi is an Iranian immigrant who had an extremely successful career in the technology industry. He is the founder of Code.org, a non-profit group that advocates computer science training and provides coding curriculum for schools around the country. Code.org is backed by companies including Google, Facebook, and Microsoft. In an interview with the NY Times, Partovi said, "I believe schools should be mandated to teach computer science. You would never send your child to a school that didn't teach math. In the 21st Century, computer science is as important as Biology. Understanding photosynthesis or H20 or electricity is just as foundational as understanding how the internet works or what an algorithm is. These things are impacting our daily lives, we need future lawyers and doctors and politicians to all understand it. We're not trying to prepare kids for jobs, we're trying to prepare kids for life. (35)

** What's the Science **

Did you know that Ayush Kumur is a 10-year-old App maker?

Apple stages a scholarship contest, which brings in students from around the world to attend its worldwide developers' conferences. Apple Scholarship contest offers young App makers a free WWDC 19 ticket (which goes for $1000) and lodging for the conference, as well as one year of memberships in the Apple developers' program. The minimum age to enter is 13, however, Ayush Kumar was so good at coding that Apple made an exception. To get accepted, he created a physics-based app with "a catapult lever that you release to fire a projectile." It was inspired by a 4th grade science project he created to explore his love of physics. The app has been submitted to the Apple App Store and he doesn't even own an I-phone. (36)

29. Why must one be conscious of the power of one's thoughts?
Optimistic thinking gives you the energy and motivation to bring your thoughts into existence. You are believing that you can achieve your goal is the first step to accomplishing it. Your actions are your thoughts manifested. When your thoughts are pessimistic your mind produces diseased seeds, which is manifested into diseased actions which brings dis-ease to your life.

30. Why must one learn the power to will?

"Champions aren't made in gyms. Champions are made from something they have deep inside them—a desire, a dream, a vision...they must have the skill and the will. But the will must be stronger than the skill." -Muhammad Ali (37)

Will- self-determination that develops into a conscious power to control one's actions or emotions.

Power = Knowledge + Force + Energy living according to the truth

When you will something into existence, that's mental power manifested.

The survival of harsh circumstances can develop will power that allows one to approach future roadblocks with confidence. This increases your chances of success.

31. Will you tell us how did I get to hell and how do I get the hell out?

Because we view history from a Euro-centric perspective, we operate without the knowledge of who we are thus we live life without purpose, identity, and direction. Western civilization has put us at a social and economic disadvantage that we cannot overcome because we help them destroy ourselves. The oppressor doesn't have to oppress because we oppress each other. That alone should tell us that most of us are doing the wrong things and we need to make a change (a change in our thinking!) because things are getting worse. Hell is the condition of the black family. Hell is not a place, it's a state of imperfection. Hell is poverty, addiction, incarceration, and death. The imperfect condition of my people. However, this disadvantage is not an excuse. Hardship and adversity are the foundation for which success is built. The solution is always inside the problem, we must recognize the roadblocks, so we can go around them.

32. Will you please define the two types of neighborhoods?

yes, there are two types of neighborhoods: Neighborhoods that are communities and neighbor-HOODS.

A neighborhood is a vicinity or physical place where there are people living near one another.

Community is any group of people living in the same area, having interest, work, etc. in common.

Neighborhoods that are communities consist of people who come together and organize for the betterment of the whole community. True neighborhoods are built from the ground up on land that is owned by the community or someone who has their best interest. No neighborhood will prosper on land that it does not own or control. Community is also a mindset. it's wanting for others what you want for yourself.

A significant number of black families live in neighborhoods that are not communities. Neighbor-HOODS are residential areas with lesser wealth, power, and status than communities. In neighbor-HOODS nothing is owned or controlled by the people who live there. Everything from the housing to the businesses is owned by people who live outside of the neighbor-HOOD. Therefore, Black people spend 95% of their income with people who do not support or contribute to the advancement of the neighbor-HOOD. "Strong black communities breed strong black families".

** *What's the Science* **

In the Jewish community, the dollar circulates for 20 days before it leaves the community.

White communities 17 days

Black neighborhoods 6 hours (38)

33. What are the prescribed laws of building thriving communities?
Communities are built through an educational system that teaches the science of everything in life and economical structure where the community controls 95% of the production and distribution of everything coming in and going out.

One of the most successful and wealthiest Black communities in U.S. history was Greenwood, a prosperous area in Tulsa, Oklahoma also known as (The Black Wall Street). In 1899, a successful entrepreneur named J.B. Stradford, arrived in Tulsa, and instituted an economical system of cooperative economics that would put the community on the path to financial freedom and power. Stradford advised the community to pool their resources together and support each other's businesses. He became the richest Black man in Tulsa through his rooming house, rental properties, and hotel "The Stratford" which was the largest Black-owned hotel in the U.S.

Around the same time, O.W. Gurley, a wealthy Black landowner from Arkansas moved to Tulsa. He purchased 40 acres of land which was "only to be sold to blacks." His 40 acres of land grew into a city of more than 10,000 people and contained a 35-block business district that held more than 600 black owned businesses, including 21 restaurants, 30 grocery stores, 2 newspapers, 2 movie theaters, a hospital, a bank, a post office, half a dozen private airplanes and a bus system. (39)

The visionary leadership of these men fueled the growth and development of this community. In less than 40 years from being (so-called) freed from slavery this community was able to amass and sustain wealth (on a scale that's rarely seen today). Black people must get back to learning and mastering all aspects of community for its the foundation of generational wealth.

** *What's the Science* **

On May 31, 1921, Black Wall St. came to an end. The deadliest race riot in U.S. history occurred because the arrest of a young Black man on questionable charges of assaulting a White woman. All 35 blocks of Greenwood were burnt to the ground. An estimated 300 people died and approximately 4,300 Black people were left homeless. (40)

34. What is your purpose?

"The person who fails to plant the seeds of purpose will be excluded from the fruits of achievement."

Purpose- 1. A mission or goal one intends to get or do. 2. The object for which something exists or is done.

My purpose is to be supreme.

My purpose is to be merciful and beneficent.

My purpose is to give the Earth what she needs to sustain life. To plant life giving seeds that will grow into the garden of Eden which is a community of precious fruit (children) who knows that their potential is limitless.

My purpose is to be a living manifestation of who I say I am.

My purpose is to make a self-transformation that's so powerful that it inspires other people to change.

My purpose is to build generational wealth for my family.

My purpose is to help other people find their purpose.

What's your purpose?

_____

_____

_____

35. What is your identity? (Who are you?)
Nature + Nationality = Identity

Identity - is the state or fact of being a specific person (individuality)

Nature - original man (origin of all minds)

Nationality - Nation of Gods and Earths

Identity - Asiatic black man, God of the universe

Black = dominate, Man = mind, Blackman = dominate mind

Asiatic: Asia = body, attic = mind

The body is just a conduit for which the mind expresses energy and matter.

Who am eye?

Arm-leg-leg-Arm-Head: Allah is the 3rd eye which is the mind

Eye am the highest extent of the mind (infinite consciousness).

Eye am the vessel which contains the consciousness and capabilities of the original thought that born the universe.

What is your identity?

_____

_____

_____

36. What's your direction? (Where are you going?)

"A person who is void of direction will linger in nothingness until they wither away."

Direction - 1. The line or course on which something is moving or is aimed to move. 2. Guidance or supervision of action or conduct: management.

Only when you find and fully understand your purpose and identity can you then align them, and they'll guide you in the direction of your destiny. Love. Peace. Happiness.

What's your direction?

_____

_____

_____

37. Why must one keep their mind at P.E.A.C.E?

P.E.A.C.E is freedom from unrighteous or oppressive thoughts.

P.E.A.C.E is a state of tranquility.

A P.E.A.C.E.FUL mind provides a calmness that allows one to travel through life gracefully. When your mind is absent of confusion your actions are in harmony.

The body is just a conduit for which the mind expresses energy and matter. If the mind possesses positive (peace) energy (thoughts), the body will produce P.E.A.C.E.F.U.L actions. If the mind possesses negative energy (thoughts), the body will produce negative actions.

The path to financial freedom is filled with potholes and detours. A pothole is a deep hole usually on the side of the road. A detour changes your course of direction. When you travel this path with a peaceful mind state your able to recognize the potholes and gracefully detour around them because you understand that success doesn't exist without struggle.

P.E.A.C.E!

Positive - Energy - Always - Creates - Enlightenment!!!

38. When all roads lead to hell which way do you go?

Because Black people are systematically deprived of equal educational and economic opportunities, we start life at a disadvantage. Because of the plight and condition of majority of black families, oftentimes we find ourselves in circumstances where we desire temporary relief from economic misery, but all options are bad.

"Fork in the road I'm always goin' right" -Lil' Wayne Tha Mobb (The Carter II) (41)

My understanding of these lyrics is that "goin' right" means to make a righteous choice, and if all roads lead to destruction you make your own road. Before you go against your morals and principles or do something unrighteous, make your own lane. Don't let someone else control your destiny. Every bad situation you're faced with someone else was in a similar or worse one and overcame it. We are the original people of the planet earth. We survived wars, natural disasters, slavery, chemical warfare, and oppression in every form. We are survivors it's in our genetics. Historically people have devised schemes and plans to take us off the planet. Yet we still stand strong as ever. The disadvantages that society places in front of us are no excuse for failure. You are the master of your own destiny. When you're looking for strength, look with-in and manifest out.

39. What is your reward for banking black?

"You run the checkup, but they never give you leverage." -Jay-Z, What's Free (42)

My understanding of these lyrics is that "We" as black people spend too much money outside of our community with companies and institutions that don't respect our business.

The #1 reason black businesses and black entrepreneurs fail is because their lack of access to capital. Major national banks have historically used redlining and other racial tactics to deny the black community financing. On the rare occasions when the loan is approved, only 47% of black business owners get the full amount they requested versus 76% of whites.

We must utilize the black banks. They have historically supported and invested in the black community. By placing your money in black banks, they are able to lend it out to other black businesses at an affordable rate. Also, they do the little things that matter the most, like taking extra time with you to show you where the flaws are in your business plan. If you don't qualify for credit, they'll tell you what you need to do to make your credit better.

The reward for banking black is the joy of giving back to yourself and your community. Cooperative economics gives us power. Join forces by combining your resources. Make a commitment to the future of the black community and see the benefits from the banks to the barbershops.

** *What's the Science* **

It turns out that there are already over 35 African American owned banks and credit unions in the United States where you can put your money if you find these types of efforts for financial stability and reinvestment in the Black community important.

Check out the list below!

1. Omega Psi Phi Credit Union - Lawrenceville, Georgia
2. Phi Beta Sigma Federal Credit Union - Washington, DC
3. One United Bank - Los Angeles, California

4. FAMU Federal Credit Union - Tallahassee, Florida

5. Credit Union of Atlanta - Atlanta, Georgia

6. North Milwaukee State Bank - Milwaukee, Wisconsin

7. Seaway Bank - Chicago, Illinois

8. The Harbor Bank - Baltimore, Maryland

9. Liberty Bank - New Orleans, Louisiana

10. United Bank of Philadelphia - Philadelphia, Penn

11. AL America Bank - Birmingham, Alabama

12. Broadway Federal Bank - Los Angeles, California

13. Carver State Bank - Savannah, Georgia

14. Capital City Bank - Atlanta, Georgia

15. Citizens Trust Bank - Atlanta, Georgia

16. City National Bank - Newark, New Jersey

17. Commonwealth National Bank - Mobile, Alabama

18. Industrial Bank - Washington, DC

19. First Tuskegee Bank - Tuskegee, Alabama

20. Mechanics & Farmers Bank - Durham, North Carolina

21. First Independence Bank - Detroit, Michigan

22. First State Bank - Danville, Virginia

23. Illinois Service Federal - Chicago, Illinois

24. Unity National Bank - Houston, Texas

25. Carver Federal Savings Bank - New York, New York

26. One United Bank - Miami, Florida

27. One United Bank - Boston, Massachusetts

28. Tri-State Bank - Memphis, Tennessee

29. Citizens Bank - Nashville, Tennessee

30. South Carolina Community Bank - Columbia, South Carolina

31. Columbia Savings and Loan - Milwaukee, Wisconsin

32. Liberty Bank - Baton Rouge, Louisiana

33. Liberty Bank - Kansas City, Missouri

34. Citizen Trust Bank - Birmingham, Alabama

35. Liberty Bank - Chicago, Illinois

36. Liberty Bank - Jackson, Mississippi

37. Toledo Urban Credit Union - Toledo, Ohio

38. Hill District Credit Union - Pittsburgh, Pennsylvania

40. Will you tell us why race matters even among families in the same socioeconomical class?

The Time Magazine had an article titled "The American Dream by the Numbers." In this article, it showed how economic disparities among racial groups still exist despite peoples' contrary beliefs. They analyzed data on 20 million children to examine how economic outcomes changed across generations. For ex. black children born to low-income parents have just a 2.5% chance of rising to the top fifth of the household-income distribution as adults. White children born into families with the same income are 4 times more likely to reach that threshold. (43)

These numbers exhibit the fact that race matters. When it comes to the American Dream, society provides opportunities for certain racial groups and roadblocks for others. This is why, group economics is so important because black people must provide opportunities for each other.

PART FIVE:
Actual Facts (1-20)

Actual FACTS

1. About 6% of working age (18-64 years old) Black men are currently in state, federal, or municipal jail. Compared to 2% of all men in the same age group. (1)

- Approximately 34% of black men (18-64 yrs. old) who are not incarcerated are ex-offenders. (2)

- 698 Americans are behind bars for every 100,000 residents. (3)

- The U.S. spends 87 billion per year to imprison 2-24 million people. (4)

Question: Does a criminal record make you a second-class citizen?

In the New Jim Crow, Michelle Alexander made some interesting points. She explained, "in each generation, new tactics have been used for achieving the same goals—goals shared by the founding fathers. (5)

The annihilation that the Criminal Justice system has done to the black family is parallel to the effects of slavery. The Criminal Justice System was created to re-enslave the Blackman.

- During slavery, the Americans implemented a system to break the slaves. One of the methods used to achieve this goal was to beat the Blackman to the point of death in front of the Black woman and child, but it was key to not let him die. He must live because a broken man is the best tool to use for breeding other broken men. Also, by breaking the Blackman in front of the black woman and child it shows them that the Blackman cannot protect or provide for them, thus making him obsolete.

- Today, the Blackman is removed from society during the prime of his life by the system. If he is not murdered in the streets by racist police, he is legally lynched in the courtroom. Placed in institutions that are designed to break his mind. Sentenced to terms so extensive that upon release the Blackman is broken, damaged, or he will lack the moral compass to journey within the boundaries of success, thus making him obsolete.

By removing the Blackman from society during the prime of his life (18-64), it directly effects the black family. It stops the Blackman from reproducing by removing the father from the home. The black woman must carry the extra burden of taking care of the family and endure the harsh reality of being black in America by herself. The objective is to create an unbalance in the black family, just as it was done in slavery by separating the parents from the children.

Rights of a slave: "Zero", can't vote, unpaid labor, not allowed to read, 3/5 of a citizen.

Rights of a felon: Denied the right to vote, unemployment discrimination, income/wage disparity (all black people), education discrimination, 3/5 of a citizen.

There's not much of a difference between the rights of a slave and the rights of a felon. Meek Mill expressed it perfectly in his song Trauma: "The 13th Amendment do not say that we are kings, it says that we are legally slaves if we go to the Bing!" (6) Prison is just another form of slavery and part of getting you in slavery/prison they had to criminalize our culture. Research shows that white people are more likely to and in general commit more crimes. However, society creates a narrative that all blacks are criminals, therefore police target, harass, and murder black people because of racial bias. The Criminal Justice System who incarcerates black men at disproportionately higher rates than whites and the sentencing disparities, clearly reflect the goals of the founding fathers to keep Black people powerless, mentally dead, and slaves.

- President A. Lincoln, debate with Stephen Douglas; Charleston 1858:

"I have no purpose to introduce political and social equality between the white and black people..."

"That I am not nor ever been in favor of making voters or jurors of negroes, nor of qualifying them to hold office nor to intermarry with white people; and I will say in addition to this, that there is a physical difference between the two which, in my judgment will probably forever forbid their living together upon the footing of a perfect equality, and in as much as it becomes a necessity that there must be a difference, I am in favor of the race to which I belong having the superior position. (7)

- President Reagan, a belief reported by Ernest W. Lefever, a nominee of Reagan for Assistant Secretary of State for Humanitarian Affairs, according to both of his brothers John and Donald (NY Times 6-4-81): "...Blacks are genetically less intelligent than whites..." (8)

2. Why don't black people read?

The condition of black people in America today can be attributed to several factors. However, the foundation of our predicament is a derivative of the American experience. Reading has been a crime for black people in America much longer than it has been legal. The Americans understood that if we knew how to read, we would learn the truth. We would learn that we taught the world how to read. This was why it was so important for the Americans to kill or separate the adults from the babies, because the adults knew their true culture. The babies were born into slavery, so they were taught that they were always slaves. And the first book they gave to the babies was the Bible. A beautiful liberating book when it's properly understood; however, the Americans used it to manipulate the babies by giving them false interpretations, that we were a cursed people and that we were meant to be slaves. Even today most black children grew up in a household where the only book is the Bible. Also, most black parents teach it to their children from a Eurocentric perspective.

Mind power is infinite and limitless, nevertheless, the brain is a muscle and just like other muscles when it's not being used or mis-used, it becomes dormant. Reading is a mental workout. It's like running on a treadmill with your thoughts. Reading is learning, learning is knowledge, and wisdom is the application of knowledge. So, to become wise, you must read.

Today, no laws exist to prevent black people from reading; still and all, policies and practices are in place to keep families of color in conditions of poverty, unable to afford books, and other educational materials to prepare our babies for academic success. Children of color have a reading proficiency significantly lower than whites. (9) This is because most students of color attend schools that lack resources, experienced teaching, and support staff that are typical of schools that primarily serve white students. (10)

There's an old saying, "if you want to hide something from a black person, put it in a book." That statement bears truth. The laws that prevented black people from reading have been abolished a long time ago, yet our reading levels and reading in general are lower than any other race in America. This is because the effect of the American experience was so damaging to the mind of black people that we no longer need a law to stop us from reading. We stop ourselves!

3. How many black billionaires are there on the planet?
According to Forbes, as of March 2020, there are 2,095 billionaires on the planet, and 14 of them identify as being of African descent. That's 1.5%.

    a. Nigeria's Aliko Dangote is currently the wealthiest Black person in the world with a fortune estimated at $8.3 billion. He started out in business more than 3 decades ago by trading in commodities like flour, sugar, and cement with a loan he received from his uncle. He went on to build Dangote Group, the largest industrial conglomerate in west Africa. His most ambitious project to date is a private oil refinery in Nigeria which is expected to reduce Nigeria's dependence on oil imports. (11)

These are the remaining Black billionaires:

    b. Mike Adenuga, Nigerian
       $5.6 billion, oil, telecoms
       Nigerian-born Adenuga is the world's 2nd richest black person. He built his fortune in oil and mobile telecoms. He is also the founder of Globacom, a Nigerian mobile phone network that has more than 40 million subscribers.

    c. Robert F. Smith, American
       $5 billion, Private Equity
       Smith is the founder of private equity firm Vista Equity Partners. The firm focuses exclusively on investing in software

companies. His multi-billion-dollar fortune was built through this firm. Also, Smith is a serial philanthropist. One of his most generous acts was when he paid off the student loans of Morehouse College's class of 2019. He later expanded the gift to cover the graduates' parents' educational debt.

d. David Steward, American
$3.5 billion, Tech
Steward is the co-founder and chairman of (IT) Provider worldwide whose customers include Citi, Verizon, and the federal government.

e. Abdulsamad Rabiu, Nigerian
$2.9 billion, cement/sugar
Rabiu is the founder of BuaGroup, a Nigerian conglomerate with interests in sugar refining, cement production, real estate, steel, port concessions, manufacturing, oil, gas, and shipping. He got his start in business working for his father, Isyaku Rabiu, a successful businesswoman from Nigeria's north region.

f. Oprah Winfrey, American
$2.5 billion, television
Oprah is still the richest African American woman in the world thanks to her daytime TV show and earnings from her Harpo Production Company. Oprah is also one of America's most generous philanthropists.

g. Michael Jordan, African American
$2.1 billion, athlete/investing

Jordan is one of the greatest basketball players and one of the highest paid. Jordan earned $1.4 billion before taxes from corporate sponsorship during his professional basketball career. His biggest investment, the Charlotte Hornets, accounts for most of his wealth.

h. Michael Lee-chin, Canadian
$2 billion, investments
Lee-chin, a Canadian of Jamaican origin, made a fortune investing in financial companies. He owns a 65% stake in National Commercial Bank Jamaica.

i. Isabel Dos Santos, Angolan
$1.4 billion, investments
Santos is the oldest daughter of Angola's former president, Jose Eduardo Dos Santos. Her multibillion-dollar wealth has come from her impressive investment portfolio, which includes a 25% stake in Angolan mobile phone company, Unitel and a 25% stake in Angolan bank Banco Bicsa. Also, a substantial stake in NOS SGPS, a Portuguese cable tv company and just under 20% of Banco BPI, one of Portugal's largest publicity traded banks.

j. Patrice Motsepe, South African
$1.4 billion, mining
Motsepe is South Africa's first and only black billionaire. He is the founder of African Rainbow Minerals (ARM), a Johannesburg stock exchange-listed mining company that has platinum nickel, chrome, iron, manganese, coal, copper, and gold. He also owns a large stake in African Rainbow capital,

a private equity firm focusing on investments in the financial services sector.

k. Strive Masiyiwa, Zimbabwean
$1.1 billion, Telecoms
Masiyiwa is the founder of Econet one of the leading mobile telecom companies in Africa. It has more than 10 million subscribers spread across Zimbabwe, Botswana, Burundi, and Lesotho.

l. Folorunsho Alakija, Nigerian
$1.1 billion, oil
Nigeria's first female billionaire is the founder of Famfa Oil, a Nigerian company that owns a substantial participating interest in OML 127, a lucrative oil block on the Agbami deep-water oilfield in Nigeria.

m. Mohammad Ibrahim, Sudanese
$1.1 billion, Mobile telecoms and investment
Sudanese-born Ibrahim founded Celtel International in 1998, one of the first mobile phone companies serving Africa and the Middle East. In 2005, he sold his company to Kuwait's mobile telecommunications company for 3.4 billion.

n. Shawn (Jay-Z) Carter, African American
$1 billion, Rap/Investments
Brooklyn-born Jay-Z is hip-hop's first billionaire. A large portion of his wealth comes from his business ventures. His Armand de brignac (Ace of Space) which he owns 100% of is worth $310 million. That, along with D'usse, his streaming service Tidal, art collections, real estate, record label, cash

investments, and his music catalog combined got him a billion dollars.

When one attempts to travel the coarse road of success adversity and failure are inevitable. This list of billionaires was not exempt. The difference between them and the average person who wants to acquire wealth is that when they encountered failure they learned from their mistakes and tried harder. When a window of opportunity came, they recognized it and maximized it. These are character qualities that help a person persevere through to success.

When you want to accomplish something, study a person who was successful at it.

** *What's the Science* ** (12)

The 14 billionaires have a combined net worth of over 34 billion.

8 are from Africa; 5 out of the 8 are from Nigeria.

5 are from America; 1 from Canada.

3 women; 11 men

11 of the 14 have 3-5 streams of income.

All gained wealth from either commodity, investments, tech, entertainment, or a combination of them all. Forbes finalized this list March 18, 2020. Just a few days after the Global Equity Market exploded due to the COVID 19 pandemic. Twelve days earlier there were 226 more billionaires in the world.

* Bonus *

At the time of this writing, Kanye West became a billionaire. Forbes estimates his net worth at 1.3 billion. According to Forbes, most of his wealth comes from his street wear brand Yeezy, which sells clothing and sneakers in a partnership with Adidas.

In 2016, Kanye tweeted that he was 53 million in debt and asked Facebook founder Mark Zuckerberg to invest 1 billion in his "ideas." Now he's the 15th member of the Black Billionaires Club.

4. If someone gave you $100, how would you spend it?
Across 14 African countries, young adults were asked this question and around half of them said they would use it to start a business. 16% said they would invest the hypothetical $100 in their education. Another 16% said they would spend it on goods or leisure and 13% said they would save the $.

The study revealed the eagerness of young adults in Africa to be self-made. In Malawi and Togo, 9 out of 10 young adults said that they intended to start a business in the next 5 years. Also, social entrepreneurship was a popular theme. According to the survey, 63% of the young adults said their idea for a business or social enterprise would benefit those living in their community. This level of social consciousness and entrepreneur mindset of young people in Africa reflects the 8 out of 14 billionaires being from that continent. This type of entrepreneur mentality is key to building wealth. (13)

5. How many Black families in America have a wealth level above a million dollars?
Out of 20 million black families, 380,000 have a net worth of above 1 million dollars. That's 1.9%.

13 million white families are millionaires. That's 15% of the white family population. Of the 13 million, 870,000 have a net worth above 12 million dollars. (14)

*** What's the Science ***

The percentage of Black and Hispanic households worth more than one million has remained under 2% since 1992. (15)

6. How many black households are in the 1% of the nation's net worth?

There are around 120 million households in America. 14 million black, 83 million white. There are 1.2 million households in the top 1% of the nation's wealth. 1.4% of them are black (16,800). 96% are white (1,152,000).

The top black households in the 1% have a median net worth of $1.2 million, whereas the top white households have a median net worth of $8.3 million. (16)

7. To be in the top 5% of black households what must your net worth be?

A black household would need a net worth of $356,000. That means that only 720,000 black households out of 14 million represent the top 5%. In contrast, white households with the same $356,000 in net worth, represent nearly 30% of the 83 million population of white households. (17)

Nearly 25 million white households have a net worth of at least $356,000 compared to 720,000 black households. The racial wealth gap is real. (18)

8. How does the top wealthiest 5% of Black America invest?

According to Harvard Business Review, the top wealthiest 5% of Black Americans are more likely to invest in more "conservative" investments, such as real estate, CD's, savings accounts, and life insurance. Compared to their white counterparts who hold more assets in stocks, bonds, and business equity ownership; investments which provide higher rewards for taking on more risk.

The explanation for this passive approach to investing is that most of todays' wealthy black people are first generation rich and 93% self-made. Compared to their white counterparts, which 40% have received some type of inheritance. (19)

** *What's the Science* **

The top 10% of households own most of the business equity, stocks, and investment real estate. When it comes to stock ownership, the top 10% owns 84% of the market. (20)

9. How long does it take to become a millionaire?

According to financial expert Chris Hogan, it took most millionaires an average of 28 years to hit the million-dollar mark. The age most of them reached that milestone was 49.

The average person's perception of a million dollars is that it's not a lot of money and it's easy to make. However, that's not reality. A million dollars is a lot of money and it takes decades of working, saving and investing to become a millionaire. (21)

10. How does education correlate with wealth?

Most high paying jobs require high levels of education. So, the more education you receive, the higher your chances of becoming a millionaire. However, there's a drastic disparity in the probability when races are compared.

An Asian with a bachelor's degree has roughly a 17% chance of becoming a millionaire. For Hispanics with a master's degree, the chance for reaching millionaire status is roughly 11%.

A white person with a master's degree has a 37% probability to become a millionaire. Blacks with a master's degree only have a 7% chance of becoming a millionaire. You'd think that people with similar educational attainment would have similar financial and career opportunities, but the numbers say otherwise. (22)

** What's the Science **

Black households headed by a college graduate have a 30% lower net worth than white households headed by someone without a degree. (23)

11. Would you tell us why anything you can't take through the 5 senses is a misconception?
"Anything outside of the laws of physics is an opinion!"

If you can't see, smell, taste, touch or hear it, it doesn't exist.

There is no such thing as luck, chance, or coincidence. They are false ideas (misconceptions).

The universe is governed by mathematics, and where mathematics reigns supreme inconsistency cannot exist!

12. Could you tell us the correlation between education and prison?

Facts:

Higher education correlates with higher wages.

Less education correlates with lower wages.

"Education that teaches you to be self-sufficient creates entrepreneurs"

Most public schools are poorly funded, so they are at a disadvantage compared to schools that have the finances to provide a proper education.

The better the education one has, the better decisions one makes.

These statistics show and prove the statement:

- 66% of state prison inmates haven't graduated from high school. (24)

- Black men ages 20-24 without a high school diploma are more likely to be in jail or prison than they are to have a job. (25)

The correlation between education and prison is that the less education you have the higher your chances are of going to prison. So why does America spend more on its prison system than it does on public schools? {The U.S. spends more on prisons and jails than it does on educating children—and 15 states spend at least $27,000 more per prisoner than they do per student. This map breaks down the spending for those states, per student and per inmate, plus the difference between the two figures.} (24) While it may seem that prison spending and education spending are unrelated, this chart proves otherwise.

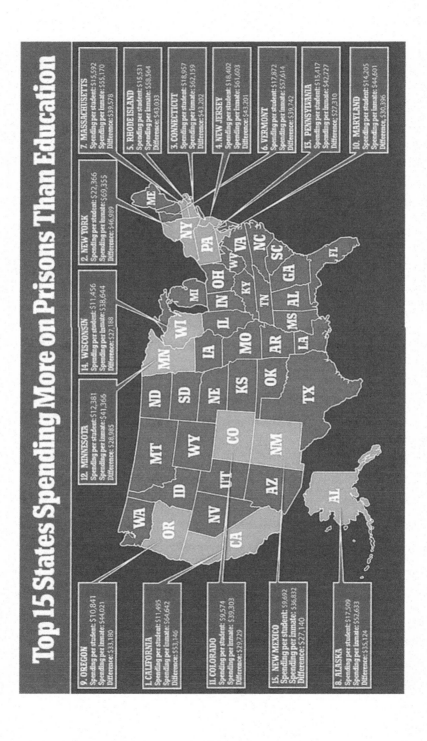

Top 15 States Spending More on Prisons Than Education

7. MASSACHUSETTS
Spending per student: $15,592
Spending per inmate: $55,170
Difference: $39,578

5. RHODE ISLAND
Spending per student: $15,531
Spending per inmate: $58,564
Difference: $43,033

3. CONNECTICUT
Spending per student: $18,957
Spending per inmate: $62,159
Difference: $43,202

4. NEW JERSEY
Spending per student: $18,402
Spending per inmate: $61,603
Difference: $43,201

6. VERMONT
Spending per student: $17,872
Spending per inmate: $57,614
Difference: $39,742

13. PENNSYLVANIA
Spending per student: $15,417
Spending per inmate: $42,727
Difference: $27,310

10. MARYLAND
Spending per student: $14,205
Spending per inmate: $44,601
Difference: $30,396

2. NEW YORK
Spending per student: $22,366
Spending per inmate: $69,355
Difference: $46,989

14. WISCONSIN
Spending per student: $11,456
Spending per inmate: $38,644
Difference: $27,188

12. MINNESOTA
Spending per student: $12,381
Spending per inmate: $41,366
Difference: $28,985

9. OREGON
Spending per student: $10,841
Spending per inmate: $44,021
Difference: $33,180

1. CALIFORNIA
Spending per student: $11,495
Spending per inmate: $64,642
Difference: $53,146

11. COLORADO
Spending per student: $9,574
Spending per inmate: $39,303
Difference: $29,729

15. NEW MEXICO
Spending per student: $9,692
Spending per inmate: $36,832
Difference: $27,140

8. ALASKA
Spending per student: $17,509
Spending per inmate: $52,633
Difference: $35,124

13. Will you please define passive income?

Passive income is money earned with minimal physical activity through a variety of ventures.

Two ways to earn passive income:

A. Index funds: Mutual funds that have a portfolio matching that of a broad-based portfolio. This may include the Dow Jones Industrial Average, Standard & Poors 500 Index, or the New York Stock Exchange, to name a few. You will be investing in the general market, not an individual stock. This passive way of investing is low risk due to the diversification of the index. This method of investing requires no physical labor, you can make money in your sleep.

B. Start a blog; blogs are cheap and highly scalable way to create passive income. You could start a blog for just a couple dollars a month. Blogs make money from advertisements and subscriptions. The bigger the audience, the bigger the check!

14. Is home ownership a key ingredient in building wealth?

Yes, home ownership is a fundamental element of building wealth. Most Black families cannot afford to buy homes because of the low wages they earn, cannot keep pace with rising home prices that continue to rise further out of budget.

- 74% of white families own a home; only 44% of black families own a home. And black family homes are less likely to appreciate in value, according to a McKinsey report.

The discrepancy in home ownership is rooted in the not-too-distant past: from 1934 to 1962, more than 98% of federally backed mortgages went to white borrowers. (27)

15. How and why are people of color being victimized by the health care system?

Historically, Black people in America have received insufficient healthcare. This is a product of systematic racism, which has led to abuse and unethical medical experimentation, for example:

- The Tuskegee Syphilis experiment (1932-1972) - Dozens of Black men died when they were deliberately infected with syphilis. Their families also became infected.

- In 2015, the Center for Disease Control hid test results from black parents of an experimental measles vaccine that showed an increased likelihood of black children developing autism. (28)

To prevent this victimization, we must develop more medical professionals. Black people must pursue careers in health and science to provide better health care and safeguard our community.

- Black people are extremely underrepresented in our nation's medical schools. Only 7.7% in 2016. This percentage must drastically grow if we want to prevent neglect of our communities. (29)

** *What's the Science* **

Black people have been pioneers in the health and science industries but many of their accomplishments have been hidden or overlooked.

Here a few of the many African Americans who made groundbreaking achievements in the health and science fields. (30)

James McCune Smith (1837) - First African American man to earn a degree in medicine and to publish articles in a U.S. medical journal;

denied college admission in America, he moved to Scotland and earned his degree.

Rebecca Lee Crumpler - First African American woman physician in the U.S. She graduated in 1864 from medical school.

Hadiyah Nelson Green - Medical physicist who recently developed groundbreaking cancer treatment using nanotechnology lasers that single out cancerous cells instead of attacking healthy ones as well (2016).

Tony Hansberry - As a 14-year-old intern practicing on mannequins, he developed a new way to stitch the vaginal cuff following surgeries and hysterectomies that cut operating time by 1/3, named the Hansberry stitch (2007).

Dr. Sebi - Identified as the greatest healer since Imhotep. He was an herbalist, pathologist, biochemist, and naturalist that specialized in natural cures for diabetes, lupus, AIDS, leukemia, sickle cell anemia, and other diseases during the late 20th century.

16. What was the financial state of the black family directly after the civil war?

The close of the civil war brought so-called freedom to nearly 4 million black people. Although this liberation was gratifying, 99% of the black families had little or no wealth, so many were in a state of uncertainty.

President Lincoln promised reparations, but after he was assassinated, Vice President Andrew Johnson reneged on the promise. So instead of complaining or waiting for crumbs to fall from the wealthy man's table, newly freed black people built an economical structure of their own. They worked extremely hard sharecropping, saving, and combining resources to build thriving black communities throughout the south.

In a 55-year period (1865-1920) they went from owning zero acres of land to owning 16 million. (Only 10% of the population at the time, yet 14% of southern farm owners) (31) All of this was accomplished amidst unimaginable discrimination and racial violence.

17. What were the methods used to stop black progress?
The US Department of Agriculture (USDA) played a significant role in the massive transfer of wealth from black to white farmers.

At the height of the national farm crisis, the (USDA) loaned billions of dollars to ensuring the survival and profit of white farmers. When it came to black farmers, they consistently discriminated, by deliberately denying loans and services, preventing upkeep and profits from the land, forcing foreclosures, tax sales and bankruptcies.

This is just an example of one of the many ways that life and wealth was stolen from the black family. Today's wealth gap is a direct reflection of the (USDA) rampant discrimination.

** *What's the Science* ** (32)

In 1984-85, the (USDA) loaned $1.3 billion to 16,000 farmers to help keep their land during the national farm crisis. Only 209 were black.

In 1920, Black people had 16 million acres of land and there were 1 million black farmers. Today, Black people own 2.3 million acres and there are only 18,000 black farmers. A loss of 85% and 98%.

18. Who are the black inventors who designed new technology that currently makes the world run more efficiently?
There are thousands of black inventors who made products or new technology that moved the world forward. Here are a few recent ones:

- Dr. Marian R. Croak: Dr. Croak holds over 200 patents with the majority related to voice-over internet protocol (VOIP). VOIP is the tech that converts your voice into a digital signal allowing you to make a call directly from a computer, VOIP phone or other data driven devices. With this, she helped advance technology surrounding calling and texting on cell phones. (33)

- Janet Emerson Bashen: In 2007, she became the first black woman to receive a software patent. The patented software Linkline is a web-based application for equal employment opportunity, claim tracking, claim management, and document management. (34)

19. What are the total number of black engineers, physicians, and lawyers?

There are more than 96,000 engineers, 41,000 physicians, and 47,000 lawyers. (35)

** *What's the Science* **

1.8 million Black people age 25 and older had an advanced degree in 2014. (Masters, Ph.D., MD, or JD) in 1995 only 677,000 of Black people had this level of education. (36)

47% of black women entering college complete a 4-year degree while only 36% of black men. (37)

Education is power so the institutions that teach and cultivate the minds of our children should be regarded as sanctuaries. (HBCU's) produce most black professionals, however I feel that these schools are underused and undervalued...

Through Historically Black Colleges and Universities (HBCU's) black people can acquire the power to reverse the poverty-stricken condition of majority of the black families in America.

There are 107 HBCU's in America who enroll 228,000 primarily black students, annually. The majority of the students come from low-income households and are the first in their family seeking a college education. Most of the schools are underfunded with little or no state support. (38)

Systemic oppression and racism are synonymously felt by black people and our educational institutions. This is not a coincidence; it's done by design to counter the barriers that society places in front of us we must unify our minds and efforts.

Food for Thought: In my opinion if the top black athletes in the country went to HBCU's instead of predominately white schools it would shift a significant portion of economic power to the Black family. Predominantly white institutions make billions of dollars off our precious young athletes, from TV deals, ticket sales, to apparel, they profit off the likeness of the Black athlete, yet no funds are given to the athlete nor the communities where they come from. This is because many if not all have historically oppressed black people and continue to this very day. Most predominately white schools have confederate flags or statutes of slave owners on campus. They have fans and mascots who dress up as confederate colonels. Also, alumni who fly confederate flags over the stadium on game day. If the top black athletes enrolled at HBCU's the billions of dollars from sports will shift to schools who give back to the black communities. Schools that we built to educate ourselves because we were not welcome at white schools. America has given us nothing, yet we give them everything and reap no real benefit. Black people in and around sports have transcended it to the billion-dollar industry it is today.

Wherever the black athlete goes, the money will follow. With the money, HBCU's will be properly funded. This will enable them to provide a better education, living conditions, and facilities for the students. By top black athletes attending HBCU's, the coaches and staff will be recognized and rewarded for their success. They will be recruited by the professional leagues or other colleges for the high paying jobs that blacks rarely obtain. All the benefits that the white schools receive from the black athlete will go to HBCU's.

Many blacks feel that the key to true equality in America is to fix the system because they feel that the system is broken. I view things differently. The system is working perfectly if you understand what it was designed to do. What people lose consciousness of is the fact that the founding fathers were extremely racist. (This is not my opinion; a thorough study of American history will exhibit these facts). The founding fathers created the system to destroy the black family and uplift the white. Many people will disagree, but again, a thorough study of history will show and prove the truth. This is just a method that I feel will be effective in the process of achieving wealth for all black families.

20. Who and what are "The Henry Baker Papers"?

Henry Baker was an African American who worked for the U.S. Patent Office during the late 1800's.

During this time, African Americans had little or no rights which made entering into contractual and legal agreements nearly impossible. Especially those of contest against white persons concerning ownership and patent infringement.

Most African American inventors never gained legal rights to their inventions and the few who did obtain patents, were rarely recognized.

Mr. Baker took it upon himself to make sure that African Americans who were rewarded patents would be "unofficially" documented. When African Americans submitted patents to the Patent Office, Mr. Baker would make a mark (only recognizable by him) on the forms.

Using these marked forms, he compiled one of the most important records in African American history. These documents became known as "the Henry Baker Papers." Without them, we would never have known the magnitude of African American contribution to the world. (39)

** *What's the Science* ** (40)

African American inventors and their inventions that you would not know about if it was not for Henry Baker.

INVENTOR / INVENTION / DATE

- John, Standard/Refrigerator/7-14-1891
- E.W. Stewart/Punching machine/5-3-1887
- William H. Richardson/child's carriage/6-18-1889
- E.R. Robinson/electric railway trolley/9-19-1893
- Newman R. Marshman/typewriting machine/4-7-1885
- Garret A. Morgan/traffic signal/11-20-1923
- Lewis Nichols Latimer/electric lamp/9-13-1881
- R.F. Flemmings Jr./guitar/3-3-1886
- J. Gregory/motor/4-26-1887
- John Albert Burr/lawn mower/5-9-1899
- A.B. Blackburn/railway signal/1-1-1888

GLOSSARY

Abstinence: [L ab(s) - from + tenere, to hold]
1) To voluntarily do without; 2) abstaining from some or all food, liquor, etc.

Abstract: [L ab(s)-, from + trahere, to draw]
1) Thought of apart from material objects;
2) expressing a quality so thought of.

Adverse: 1) Opposed, unfavorable.

Advocate: [L ad, to + vocare, to call]
One who speaks or writes in support of another or a cause

African American: A member of the Black race who was born in America.

Aristocratic: [Gr. aristos, best + kratos, to rule]
1) Government by a privileged minority, usually of inherited wealth.
2) Privileged ruling class or upper class

Alkebulan: One of the original names of Africa. The Greeks and Romans renamed the continent Africa.

Beneficent: Showing beneficence; doing or resulting in good.

Black: Dominate, original, father of all races. All people of color, all life came from blackness.

Born: To be brought into existence, to be complete mentally as well as physically.

Build: To construct, to add on.

Capital: Money or property owned or used in business assets.

Cipher: Complete circle 360 degrees. 120 degrees knowledge. 120 degrees wisdom, and 120 degrees understanding.

Civilization: 1) One having knowledge, wisdom, understanding, culture, and refinement and is not a savage in the pursuit of happiness. 2) A civilizing or being civilized. 3) The total culture of a people

Conglomerate: A large corporation formed by merging many diverse companies.

Crystallize: To take on or cause to take on a definite form.

Culture: A natural way of life.

Cyclical: Of or having the nature of a cycle; occurring in cycles.

Derivative: Derived, specif. not original or novel. Something derived.

Destroy: To ruin, to take away completely.

Diaspora: The migration or scattering of a people away from an ancestral homeland.

Dormant: 1) Inactive 2) In a resting or torpid state

Empower: To give authority or power to. Also enable.

Entrepreneur: [Fr. entreprendre to undertake] one who organizes and assumes the risk of a business or enterprise.

Equality: Is to deal equally with all human families on the planet earth. Equality means to be equal in everything.

Eurocentric perspective: When a person's understanding of life is rooted from a European point of view.

Ethnicity: [ME, heathen, fr. LL ethnicus, fr GK ethnikos national, gentile, for ethnos nation, people] of or relating to races or large groups of people classed according to common traits and customs.

Ethnic: A member of a minority ethnic group who retains its customs, language, or social views.

Etymology: The history of a linguistic form (as a word) shown by tracing its development and relationships.

Fortify: [L fortis, strong + facere, to make] to strengthen or enrich physically, emotionally, etc.

Fortitude: [L. fortis, strong] strength of the mind that enables one to meet adversities with courage.

Freedom: 1) means to free your dome from mental death. 2) the quality or state of being free.

God: Asiatic Blackman. The supreme being who is the sole controller of the universe.

Heaven: Is not a place, it's a state of existence. Heaven is love, peace and happiness.

Hell: Is a state of imperfection.

Inferiority complex: An unconscious impulse or behavior that one is of lesser quality, importance, or value.

Jim Crow: Torture and or discrimination against Black people, esp. by legal enforcement or traditional sanctions.

Justice: A reward or penalty for one's actions or deeds.

Knowledge: Means to look, listen, and observe things for what they are instead of what they seem to be. Knowledge means to know the ledge, so you won't fall off the edge.

Leverage: Borrowed funds for business venture to enhance return or value without increasing investment.

Liberate: [L liber, free] freedom or release from slavery or oppression.

Longevity: [L longus, long + aevum, age] Long life.

Love: The highest level of understanding.

Manifest: To make evident or certain by showing or displaying.

Master: Is one who knows or understands a particular field or study.

Melanin: [Gr melas, black] Production of melanocyte cells which are pigment forming cells. Melanin is a substance found in practically all living organisms. Dark color or pigment of the human body that is found internally as well as externally. The external melanin is found in the hair, eyes, and skin, which absorbs and converts various forms of electromagnetic energy (sunlight) into energy states that can be used by the nervous system.

Mental state: Condition of one's mind.

Meritocratic (meritocracy): A system in which the talented are chosen and moved ahead based on their achievements.

Minuscule: Exceedingly small

Misnomer: [OFr mes, mis + nomer, to name] a wrong name.

Monetize: of or relating to making money from something.

Nationality: 1) Membership in a particular nation. 2) A people having a common origin, tradition, and language and capable of forming a state. 3) A legal relationship involving allegiance of an individual and protection on the part of the state.

Nature: [L natura, to be born] 1) The inherent quality or basic constitution of a person or thing, 2) One's natural instincts or way of life.

Nourishment: 1) Food, nutrient 2) The action or process of growth and development.

Optimal: Most desirable or satisfactory.

People of Color: Everybody that's non-white.

Philanthropy: 1) Good will toward all people. 2) Charitable act or a gift.

Photosynthesis: the process by which chlorophyll-containing plants make carbohydrates from water and from carbon dioxide in the air in the presence of light.

Pillage: [MFr piller, to rob] 1) A plundering 2) Goods stolen or taken by force

Plagiarism (plagiarize): To take (ideas, writings, etc.) from another and pass them of as one's own.

Poverty-stricken: The condition or quality of being extremely poor.

Pseudoscience: [Gr pseud in, device] A theory, Methodology or practice purported to be scientific.

Racial parameters: Expectations or limits regarding one's potential based on racist views or ideas.

Refinement: 1) Means to be cleansed mentally as well as physically, 2) The process of being made free from impurities and purified.

Righteous: [alteration of right wise, right + wise] 1) Acting in a just, upright manner; virtuous, 2) Morally right or justifiable. Being righteous has nothing to do with religion.

Second Class Citizen: 1) A member of a state or nation who has zero or partial civil rights due to the systemic racism of a country. 2) People who the government and the citizens who lie therein deem as inadequate and inferior in the social, economic, and racial class of a country.

Socioeconomic: 1) Of or involving both social and economic factors. 2) The social structure within economics.

Strenuous: requiring or characterized by great efforts or energy.

Supreme: [L superius, that is above] highest in quality

Third eye: [The mind] the pineal gland which is in the center of the brain mass is considered the 3rd eye. In Hindu tradition it is represented with a dot in the center of the forehead. It was also earlier recognized by ancient Egyptians, depicted as the uraeus (a serpent shown rising from the forehead), or the udjat, also known as the eye of Horus. The pineal gland is activated by light, ideally sunlight, and it controls the various biorhythms of the body.

Tranquility: [tranquillus] A state of peacefulness. Calm, serene.

Understanding: 1) Means to see clearly with your mind your 3rd eye. 2) To grasp mentally, to comprehend.

Vehemently: [L vehere, carry] 1) violent; impetuous 2) full of intense or strong passion.

Wisdom: Wisdom is the manifestation of one's knowledge. Wisdom is the action part of one's knowledge.

APPENDIX: NOTES

FOREWORD

1) Book of African American Quotations, edited by Joslyn Pine

2) Book of African American Quotations, edited by Joslyn Pine p. 177

3) Book of African American Quotations, edited by Joslyn Pine p. 82"

4) Book of African American Quotations, edited by Joslyn Pine p. 116

5) USA Today, 4/30/2019, Jay-Z performance at Webster Hall, New York

6) Book of African American Quotations, edited by Joslyn Pine, (2011) p. 164

7) Book of African American Quotations, edited by Joslyn Pine, (2011) p. 68

8) Book of African American Quotations, edited by Joslyn Pine, (2011) p. 33

9) Book of African American Quotations, edited by Joslyn Pine, (2011) p. 138

PART ONE: STUDENT ENROLLMENT

1) 2016 federal reserve survey of consumer finances, www.blackenterprise.com/habits of millionaires/the state of Americas wealthy black people by John Tucker

2) 2016 federal reserve survey of consumer finances, NYTimes 8/22/19 www.newsmax.com/antoniomoore/black millionaires-wealth-disparity/2017/10/04/black millionaires hardly exist in America.

3) Essence.com 10/2018

4) Merriam Webster Collegiate Dictionary 11 edition

5) Black demographics.com

6) Washington Post 3-2-2019

7) Pittsburgh Courier 8-20-19

PART TWO: LOST FOUND KEYS TO SUCCESS

1) Merriam Webster Collegiate Dictionary 11 edition

2) Merriam Webster Collegiate Dictionary 11 edition

3) Merriam Webster Collegiate Dictionary 11 edition

4) Essence Magazine May 2019

5) Essence Magazine May 2019

6) Rolling Stone Magazine May 2018

7) Washington Post May 20, 2019

8) NY Times March 14, 2019

9) NY Times March 14, 2019

10) Blackdemographics.com

11) Merriam Webster Collegiate Dictionary 11 edition

12) Merriam Webster Collegiate Dictionary 11 edition

PART THREE: NOURISHMENT FOR THOUGHT

1) Questions answered by SunGod Amenti, Questions asked by Self Power Allah

PART FOUR: KNOWLEDGE YOUR CULTURE CIPHER (1-40)

1) Barron Weekly: Sources: US Census; D. B. Global Research; Survey of consumer finances

2) According to Morning Star Direct

3) Barron Dictionary of Finance and Investment Terms (8th Ed.) Jordan Goodman

4) Essence Magazine May 2019

5) Techel.com, Money.com May 2019

6) NOI DVD

7) NY Times 12-23-19

8) Dr. Supreme Understanding and C'Bs Alife Allah (2012) The Science of Self p. 145

9) NY Times 7-9-19

10) Forbes Magazine 6-30-19

11) Maggie Anderson with Ted Gregory (2012) Our Black Year p. xii, 243-248

12) Maggie Anderson with Ted Gregory (2012) Our Black Year p. xii, 243-248

13) Nielsen.com article Black Impact: Consumer Categories where African Americans move markets census.gov

14) Nielsen.com article Black Impact: Consumer Categories where African Americans move markets census.gov

15) Powernomics, by Dr. Claude Anderson

16) Kite Magazine, Issue #4, Final Call Newspaper, March 2019

17) Inc. Magazine July/August 2019

18) Blackdemographics.com

19) Washington Post 10-2-19

20) Inc. Magazine September 2019

21) Merriam Webster Dictionary

22) Merriam Webster Dictionary

23) Merriam Webster Dictionary

24) Blackdemographics.com

25) Blackdemographics.com

26) Blackdemographics.com

27) McKisney Global Institute

28) Interview KBA 10-19-19

29) NY Post 10/9/19

30) Harlem Capital, Forbes.com, Mississippi Library Commission

31) The Atlantic October 2019, Article by Jamele Hill

32) The Chronicle of Higher Edu.

33) The Chronicle of Higher Edu.

34) Wallstreet Journal 11-17-19

35) NY Times 1-20-19

36) USA Today

37) African American Quotations, edited by Joslyn Pine

38) Maggie Anderson with Ted Gregory (2012) Our Black Year p. xii, 243-248

39) Hannibal B. Johnson (1998) Black Wallstreet

40) Hannibal B. Johnson (1998) Black Wallstreet p. 27-39

41) Lil' Wayne, The Mobb, Tha Carter II

42) Jay-z, What's Free, Championships

43) Time Magazine, March 2-9/2020

PART FIVE: ACTUAL FACTS 1-20

1) Blackdemographics.com

2) Blackdemographics.com

3) According to Prison Policy Initiative, nonprofit org.

4) Fortune.com, Fortune Magazine 2/1/18

5) Michelle Alexander, The New Jim Crow (2012) Introduction p. 1-3

6) Rapper Meek Mill, lyrics from his song 'Trauma'

7) What they never told you in history class, Vol. 1, by Indus Khemit Kush

8) What they never told you in history class, Vol. 1, by Indus Khemit Kush

9) Childtrends.org

10) Childtrends.org

11) Forbes.com

12) Forbes.com

13) A study conducted by international polling PBS research on the behalf of the Ichikowite Family Foundation Charity

14) www.newsmax.com/antoniomoore/black-millionaires-wealth-wealth-disparity/2017/10/04/1d/817622 Black Millionaires Hardly Exist in America

15) Washingtonpost.com

16) www.blackenterprise.com/its-lonely-at-the-top/-habits of millionaires: The State of America's Wealthy Black People by John Tucker

17) www.blackenterprise.com/its-lonely-at-the-top/-habits of millionaires: The State of America's Wealthy Black People by John Tucker

18) www.blackenterprise.com/its-lonely-at-the-top/-habits of millionaires: The State of America's Wealthy Black People by John Tucker

19) www.blackenterprise.com/its-lonely-at-the-top/-habits of millionaires: The State of America's Wealthy Black People by John Tucker

20) Barron's 6-22-20, Sources: US Census; DB Global Research; Survey of Consumer Finances.

21) www.Daveramsey.com/blog/how-many-millionaires-in-us? by Chris Hogan

22) www.financial/samurai.com/ chances-becoming-millionaire-by-race-age-education

23) Sources: St. Louis fed, Pew research center, federal reserve board survey of consumer finances

24) The Movement newspaper March-Spring issue #37. www.hrcoalition. org, www.dailymail/article-16317783/incarceration-us-education-american-spends-prison-does-public-schools.htmll.co.uk/news

25) The Movement newspaper March-Spring issue #37. www.hrcoalition. org, www.dailymail/article-16317783/incarceration-us-education-american-spends-prison-does-public-schools.htmll.co.uk/news

26) The Movement newspaper March-Spring issue #37. www.hrcoalition. org, www.dailymail/article-16317783/incarceration-us-education-american-spends-prison-does-public-schools.htmll.co.uk/news

27) The Movement newspaper March-Spring issue #37. www.hrcoalition. org, www.dailymail/article-16317783/incarceration-us-education-american-spends-prison-does-public-schools.htmll.co.uk/news

28) Black Seeds 2020 calendar, www.Blackseedsinc.org

29) Black Seeds 2020 calendar, www.Blackseedsinc.org

30) Black Seeds 2020 calendar, www.Blackseedsinc.org

31) Black Seeds 2020 calendar, www.Blackseedsinc.org

32) Black Seeds 2020 calendar, www.Blackseedsinc.org

33) Black Seeds 2020 calendar, www.Blackseedsinc.org

34) Black Seeds 2020 calendar, www.Blackseedsinc.org

35) Black Seeds 2020 calendar, www.Blackseedsinc.org

36) Black Seeds 2020 calendar, www.Blackseedsinc.org

37) Black Seeds 2020 calendar, www.Blackseedsinc.org

38) USA Today 6-10-20

39) www.smith-lenoir.com, list of known African American inventors 1845-1980

40) www.smith-lenoir.com, list of known African American inventors 1845-1980

ABOUT THE AUTHOR
SUNGOD AMENTI (ahh-mehn-tee)

In my culture, we teach that Black people are the original people of the planet earth. We teach that the Black man is God, and the Black woman is earth. Just as the sun is the center of the solar system the Black man is the center of his family. Sun, Moon, and Stars = Black man, Black woman, and Black child.

Your name defines your nature. A snake is called a snake because its sneaky, slithery, and deadly. A pig is called a pig because its nature is to be filthy. My nature is God. God is the highest extent of the mind, meaning my mind is a reproduction of the original mind that created the universe. The name my parents gave me is my honorable name but SUNGOD AMENTI is my righteous name, for it defines my nature.

Man is a replica of the sun on earth, for they possess the same powers. (The micro of the macro). The light that travels from the sun to the earth fertilizes, cultivates, and powers the planet. My light which is my intelligence fertilizes, cultivates, and powers the people around me when I give them life giving teachings shown and proved through my ways and actions.

God is the supreme being who is the sole controller of his universe.

Supreme means highest in quality, original.

Being means to exist, a living thing.

Black people are the original people of the planet earth. Everybody else was created in our likeness. Therefore, the Black man is a supreme being. (God).

AMENTI: Allah-Manifest-Everything-Naturally-Through-Intelligence

Every original man's nature is God. When God is manifested through the mind, he becomes Allah, a supreme state of existence. (example) I was born God but by me not having knowledge of self I was not able to manifest it. Therefore, I did things that went against my nature like selling drugs. So, my lack of understanding of who I am; made me manifest devilishment instead of God.

Only when a person is fully conscious of his natural state of being; can he then shape the universe with his intelligence and be the master of his own destiny.

When I did not know who I was the world was shaping me. Now that I am in the know, the world will know!